Single Mom Homeschooling

Kim Sorgius

Single Mom Homeschooling
Copyright Kim Sorgius 2014.

Dedicated to my sweet children:
Leah, Rachel, Nathan, and Luke
Who daily make this journey worth walking

Table of Contents

Introduction 1

Challenge 1: The Impossibility Naysayers 5

Just Put the Kids in School: Why that's Not Always the Best Option 5

The Legal Dilemma 12

Challenge 2: You Are Not Alone 17

Stats and Stories of Other Single Moms 23

Meet Mary Jo 28

Meet Columba 40

Meet Latoya 49

Getting the Homeschooling Support That You Need. 53

Challenge 3: Money 59

Possible Income Sources 60

Creative Cost Cutting 71

Affording Food For Your Family 78

Affording Clothes for Your Family 83

Challenge 4: Setting up Your Homeschool. 91

Writing Your Mission 96

Choosing the Right Curriculum 101

Why You Need Independent Learners. 106

How to Plan the Year 111

Organizing Your Homeschool Notebook 117

Challenge 5: Managing the Load 125

Finding a Workable Daily Schedule 125

Managing the Mess: Chores 131

Dealing with Exhaustion 139

Introduction

I picture her the same way you might: homeschooling momma driving a 15-passenger van, wearing handmade jean skirts and grinding her own wheat to bake bread. Her husband arrives home from a long day at work and leads the family in Bible reading and prayer time as they finish up a home-cooked meal. Together, the whole family cleans the kitchen as they sing praise songs. Once the baby's cloth diaper has been changed, momma plans school for the next day before she settles in with a good Bible study.

Lovely, isn't it? It's a perfect picture and not a bad thing to strive for, but it isn't always reality. When we picture homeschooling families this way, we are focusing on their ideal best day, not their everyday. We are missing the fact that real life is messy, even when you love Jesus. It's messy when you homeschool, and even when your family gathers 'round the table with a Bible in hand. The truth is, all siblings fight, good mommas burn bread, and even Christian homeschooling families walk through tragedies.

Following my husband's leadership, I began homeschooling our first child, casually, when she was 3, and was in full-swing by kindergarten. Our second child, just 13 months behind her, was usually a part of any lesson we embarked upon. I had experience as a former classroom teacher and desired greatly to homeschool with excellence. I started following blogs of large homeschooling families, reading books, and attending conventions. I started DOING all the things I thought made me a good homeschooler.

By the middle of first grade, the enemy attacked our home and everything came crashing down. Within a few months, my husband left and I was suddenly a single mom—a single homeschooling mom with a 1st grader, kindergartner, 2-year-old, and baby on the way. Without warning, all of the "perfect things" I had been doing were no longer going to work. I was convinced that homeschooling families were perfect, and for years I had been trying hard to "make" our family fit this perfect mold. Now I had no idea where to turn.

How in the world would I homeschool as a single mom? How would I have time? Wouldn't I need to work? And even if those details worked out, wouldn't others shun me? Would I be mocked and labeled as the black sheep? Surely I would be excluded. The questions went on and on for weeks, months, and even years. Somewhere in there, I was forcing homeschooling into a box, one with a closed lid that said, "Keep Out: imperfect families and single moms." I bought the lie that I wasn't perfect enough to homeschool and that my circumstances were surely going to consume the opportunity. In that place of confusion, I just pressed on with what I already knew and God leaned into my desperation. Over time, He gently taught me the truth.

As it turns out, perfect was such a crazy lie and so far from the reality of life. The perfect homeschooling family doesn't exist. God showed me that I can still homeschool in my own broken world because we are all broken, even those who aren't showing it on the outside. Once I began to believe Him, He brought amazing families, friends, and resources alongside me. More than that, once I started to believe Him, our homeschool started to thrive.

Do you find yourself with a messy, broken life? Are you desperately seeking a way to homeschool despite your imperfect circumstances? Oh friend, I wish that other circumstances had brought us together, but I have to tell you how glad I am you found your way here. I pray that in the pages of this book you will find encouragement that is beyond what you can think or even imagine (Ephesians 3:20)! I am praying for you even in this moment, believing that God will meet you here.

Homeschooling as a single mom is certainly a sacrifice. But if our eyes are fixed on Jesus, we can rest firmly in the protection and provision of our gracious God. Yes, momma may not see a lot of quiet time and will rarely go to the bathroom without an audience. But in the end, this tiny sacrifice of our life's agenda will enable our children to one day give up their lives for the ONE who gave it all up for us.

One note before you read:

The purpose of this book is to equip and encourage single moms who desire to homeschool. But, I cannot let the topic come and go without addressing the white elephant in the room. If you are reading this book looking for ammunition to help you leave your spouse/family, you've come to the wrong place. Simply put, this book is not written to give you a reason to leave your marriage. God desires that you stay and fight with all you have! I do understand that there are situations where you must leave. Of course, that is between you and God. It is just my heart's desire that this book would never be used as a catalyst for breaking up a marriage!

Challenge 1:

The Impossibility Naysayers

Just Put the Kids in School:
Why that's Not Always the Best Option

When I first became a single mom, everyone else had already made up their mind about my circumstances. I would have to get a job and put the kids in public school. There was no way to consider the idea of continuing to homeschool as a single mom. The consensus was that it would be impossible. And I almost listened to them on several occasions. Our lives had been turned completely upside down and the dread of another change was pretty much the motivating factor for continuing to homeschool those first few years.

Truthfully, it was nearly 3 years after he left before I made a conscious decision about whether or not this homeschool thing would work out. Prior to that point, we just prayed and God provided everything we needed. I did everything I could to stay out of the decision. But then one day all the legal mess was finally settled and I stared blankly at the numbers. No matter how you crunched them, I would indeed have to bring in some income. Plus, I had a serious time issue on my hands between homeschooling, mothering, managing the house, and bringing in that income. This homeschooling thing was going to need a very strong backbone if I was going to drown out the naysayers and encourage myself to stand strong. So I wrote out my defense. I didn't really write it for anyone else. I had no intention of posting it on the front door for family to read before they entered with their opinions. It was really for my own heart. It would serve its purpose as encouragement to my soul on those days when giving up seemed most logical.

Why I choose to homeschool as a single mom

1. Family unity

I knew that in the long run it wasn't money or things that kids desire which was most important; it was time. I had grown up with a single mom and I knew that time together would be scarce, making it harder to connect. I desperately wanted to know my kids, enjoy my kids, and disciple my kids. Time together as a family would always be more important than the extras, even if extras were particular types of food, brand-name clothing, larger houses, or a nice car. Homeschooling brought with it the promise of more time with my kids. I knew it meant I might have to hold a little one on my lap while I was typing. But to me that seemed so much better than sitting at a desk somewhere, typing, while that little one was in someone else's lap.

Regardless of how it happens, kids who grow up in a home without their father have deep wounds. Their very identities are questioned and the unknowns set nightmares in their hearts. They desperately need family unity. They need God's truths in their hearts and they need to be held. As the child of a single mom, I can tell you that extra time will not be found by sending the kids to school. We went to school 8 hours a day, only to return in the evening. When my mom got home from work, those evening hours were filled with homework, dinner prep, paying bills, and tackling that mountain of laundry. Quality time was scarce.

Yes, homeschooling will take time and energy, but a great homeschool curriculum can usually be done in less than 3 hours a day, leaving time for the children to help with chores and time for everyone to enjoy being together. Homeschooling our children will help foster much-needed family unity and begin to rebuild our children's identities.

2. Provide stability

Counselors agree that stability is a crucial issue for children experiencing loss (even if daddy just moved down the street). When children experience traumatic circumstances, stability becomes a necessity. If you were already homeschooling when you became a single mom, sticking with it will provide much-needed security for your precious little ones. If you were not already homeschooling, keeping them at home would be a change, but it can keep them from facing the changing tides of the school environment. This was especially true for my family in those first few years. Homeschooling provided less disruption and the necessary stability for my children. They knew what to expect of their school day, even if they didn't know if we would spend the afternoon in line at DSS or at a food bank. They knew they could depend on me to be with them every time they needed me.

3. Protect them from bullies

Just read the news and you will be mortified by the stories of bus monitor bullies and the like. Kids are mean, and the school setting cannot provide the supervision to stop it. Do you know who those bullies are picking on? Children from a broken home are much more likely to experience bullying. They bring to the table far more issues to be made fun of, such as the lack of a parent, torn or tattered clothes, free or reduced lunches, and most likely a working parent who cannot attend school functions. Believe me, I am speaking out of personal experience here. There wasn't a single year of my educational career that I wasn't picked on, even as early as kindergarten. I grew up absolutely terrified of people and without a single ounce of self-worth. I even seriously contemplated suicide multiple times as a teen. Please don't be fooled into thinking that I am the exception. Countless stories have been told of such horrific experiences in school. Of course, homeschooling will not exempt your kids from this mean behavior (unless you hide under a rock), but it will drastically decrease it. Plus, the times when your children are with other children, the adult ratio is much higher, making it easier for parents to intervene when the comments get out of hand.

4. Take breaks when YOU need them

Homeschooling will give you the opportunity to step back from learning when your children are going through a hard time (or when you simply can't get out of bed). When your heart hurts, it can be difficult to think about a math lesson. On tough days, we change plans and stay in bed with read-alouds or ipod apps. Even with taking off as many days as we needed, my kids recorded more than the required 180 days during that first school year after I became single. Had they gone to school, it is likely they would have fallen seriously behind.

5. Save money

Sending my older kids to school would cost money. Yes, going back to work would provide some income for me, but on a teacher's salary, it would hardly pay for the huge daycare and after-school care bills. Plus, even public school costs money when you calculate things like school clothes that won't get your kids beat up, supplies, lunch money, field trips and even gas to get them to school. You can actually homeschool completely for free. You will save money on more wholesome lunches and you can pick the free field trips. Of course, school clothes can even be worn out pajamas.

6. Improve Character

There is one more benefit that I could not have imagined way back then. It was in the process of coping with the circumstances that my kids became very independent and very helpful. They are now willing to eat a little less to save money. They do laundry, dishes, and clean bathrooms. You name it, the chore is on their shoulders. They have risen to the occasion and found themselves a part of the family by their ability to contribute to helping us get by.

Some would say my kids had to grow up too early, but I don't really see it that way. They are still very innocent. They still love to play, and they have more time to do it because they don't go to school. Instead of spending hours standing in line, sharpening pencils, and waiting for the teacher to discipline another student before she can begin instruction, my kids spend that time contributing to the household. It's really rather beautiful. They are gaining skills which will be incredibly useful for their entire existence as adults, not just their academic life.

When you look at all these points, working from home and homeschooling my kids brings with it the benefit of time, money, and so much more. Yes, there are some negatives and very hard challenges that come with this choice to homeschool. We will get to those later in this book. However, I think the benefits far outweigh those negative elements.

Believe me, I know what you are thinking and I agree with you. Yes, it is harder to homeschool when you are a single mom. No one comes home and changes diapers while you take a bubble bath to get away from it all. But the truth is, everything is harder when you are a single mom. It really doesn't matter what activity you are doing, you now do it without help. Don't buy the lie that you are not able to homeschool simply because he left. It is going to take some sacrifice. But being a good mom is always a sacrifice.

We must daily choose to act on behalf of our children, often setting aside our own personal agendas. Being a single homeschooling mom may be the ultimate sacrifice, but aren't they worth it? Perhaps we could have a little more money if we worked outside the home. Perhaps we could find a job that isn't as demanding. These thoughts might be reasonable, but they aren't pointing us to the real truth. This life isn't about what we can gain. This life is about serving the one who made the ultimate sacrifice for us. Yes, being a single homeschooling mom is a sacrifice. But it is a sacrifice that I am willing to make—to train them up to be like HIM because I am but a vapor, yet the legacy I leave will last an eternity. (Deut. 6) Are you in?

The Legal Dilemma

I remember the day I signed the divorce papers. The golden squares of the doors shimmered as the sun bounced in every direction. How badly I wanted to leave them closed, but I knew I could not. My hand reached out to pry open what was heavy. The ascent to the fourth floor consumed me with anxiety and my knees were so weak I could scarcely find the strength to step out of the elevator. I whispered a prayer, "Lord, I don't have the strength to even move my feet. I am depending on you to do this." All too quickly, the door of the elevator opened and my feet submitted.

As I stepped into my lawyer's office, a fresh wave of nausea rolled over me as if it were the first time. Although I knew it was in my mind, the office reeked of all things dead. I desperately wanted to flee and I know I would have if the paralegal hadn't rounded the corner. With a warm smile she handed me a tissue, "It's going to be okay." Suddenly I felt the burn of the tears streaming down my face as if they hadn't been there before. As directed, I sat in the chair and stared at the row of dark, thick law books on the shelf. Everything in this place seemed so wrong. My heart ached for the thousands of families destroyed by the piece of paper I knew I would have to sign. I lamented over the brokenness of sin and found myself longing for a time when divorce wasn't easier than buying a pair of shoes.

The paper she handed me felt so heavy that I had to sit down. Its very particles burned the tips of my shaking fingers. "It's just a piece of paper," she whispered, "I know you don't like it, but the court will order it so, even if you don't sign it." I knew she was right. My failure to sign wouldn't stop it from happening. Even though it takes two to get married, I no longer had a voice. Failure to sign would simply waive any ability to help my kids. I desperately needed the strength to help them, to protect them. That is when God got my attention. On the wall, a printout of an email boldly proclaimed:

God brought you to this place, He will bring you out.

I looked back down to a now tear-stained paper. *God will bring me out of this.* Right there in the most dreadful place I knew, God poured out His love for me, reminding me He was not absent from that place. The paper suddenly became meaningless. I knew I was in obedience and I knew He had just wrapped me in His promise. *He will bring me out. He is not going to leave me here in the desert, gasping for air. He will bring me out* (2 Timothy 4:18). Suddenly everything seemed so clear. Of course I would homeschool, and of course God would provide a way. I didn't even need to know how it would happen. All I had to do was trust.

I won't lie and tell you I wasn't afraid. I even personally knew someone who had lost the freedom to homeschool in her divorce. I was well aware that there was a possibility I would lose that freedom as well. I knew homeschooling was a privilege not everyone was afforded. I simply trusted God to do His good and perfect will in my situation. I had enough faith to believe (I mean REALLY believe) that if I was supposed to homeschool, He would take care of every detail, including the legal dilemma. And He did.

I know you are wondering, too. I know you are praying and possibly even agonizing over this dilemma. It's important that I remind you I'm not a lawyer. Nothing in this chapter can serve as legal advice for you. I would strongly urge you to seek legal counsel. Every dime you spend will be worth it. There are also places where you can get legal help without cost to you. Try contacting a local women's shelter for help. As long as you promise to remember that I'm not a lawyer, I will share with you some of my experience after praying with 1000's of women in this legal dilemma. (See stats below)

If you are already homeschooling when your marriage ends, it is very likely you will be able to continue homeschooling. Generally speaking, the judge will honor your desire to keep circumstances as normal as possible. Throwing the kids into school suddenly would not be in anyone's best interest. They call this "keeping the status quo." If you are not already homeschooling, it is possible for the father to fight your desire to do so. Sadly, he has a good chance of winning. It probably doesn't come as a surprise to you that our government isn't too quick to defend anyone's right to homeschool. (For the record, homeschool legal defense groups will not get involved in a civil matter such as this.)

In either case, it is best to work out an amicable agreement with the father. If at all possible, get permission to homeschool written in your legal agreement or divorce paperwork. Chances are, you can use this as a bargaining tool when you go to mediation. In my experience, not too many fathers expend the energy to fight this unless it somehow hurts them. This would be a good time to show how you staying home financially benefits him. For example, a full-time job outside the home would leave the children in after-school care which is rather costly. In most states, he will be responsible for a portion of that. I know that he should care more about the well-being of the children and their academic success, but sadly I don't find that to be the case. I would focus on ways it would benefit him directly.

Legal matters aside, don't discount God. If He has called you to homeschool, it doesn't matter what the stats say or what your ex-husband says. It won't matter if he says he will fight it. It won't matter that you've never homeschooled before. It only matters that God can be trusted to do exactly what He said He would do (1 Thess. 5:24)! Don't be discouraged, my friend. Keep pressing on!

The Legal Dilemma

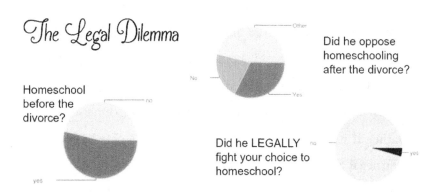

Homeschool before the divorce?

Did he oppose homeschooling after the divorce?

Did he LEGALLY fight your choice to homeschool?

Challenge 2:

You Are Not Alone

It's 10:13 pm on Friday night. You step on a handful of now-broken crayons as you fumble with the light switch. The empty house surrounds you with darkness. The kids are now with their dad and you are stranded with a stack of bills you can't pay, a filthy house, and a never-ending to-do list. You know you should get started on something or even just go to bed so you can get up early tomorrow. But the tears explode in streaks of fire down your cheeks instead. It's here in the darkness that the loneliness takes over.

My friend, do you find yourself suffocating in the emptiness?

Maybe you can't relate to the visitations or the stack of never-ending bills. But sweet single mom, I know we have this loneliness in common. In fact, it's often the very first comment we see when someone joins our single mom groups. No matter what the circumstances, the feelings of loneliness sink deep into our souls. We are certain it's not possible that anyone has ever felt this way or gone through these same things. We are certain no one is crazy enough to attempt this homeschool thing as a single mom. We are certain because we know darkness, and darkness feels lonely.

Dear Single Mom who feels alone…it's a lie.
Yep. It's a bold-faced, stupid attempt by the father of lies to kick you while you are down (John 8:44). And if you aren't intentional to defeat him, he will succeed. I can't help but think of Anna from *Frozen* as she is dancing around the lonely castle proclaiming that "for the first time in forever" she won't be alone. No more talking to the pictures on the wall. No more dark nights. But she is so wrong. Every time I hear that song I remind my kids, "She never had to be alone." By now they groan and beg me to stop telling them that. But I refuse. I refuse because I know that in our flesh we are tempted to believe this very frequent and fatal tactic of Satan to steal our joy.

Now Anna might have felt alone as there is no indication that she knew Jesus as her Savior, but it doesn't have to be that way for us. With Jesus, we are NEVER, ever alone. True, your best friend may not have walked through divorce. Your mom might not be able to relate to homeschooling. You might even live in a town miles away from another single mom or homeschooler. But you are still not alone.

Let's look at what the Bible says.

The first verse that comes to mind when people start talking about God being with us is some version of Deut. 31:8: "*It is the LORD who goes before you. He will be with you; he will not leave you or forsake you. Do not fear or be dismayed*" (ESV). I love that God promises never to leave us. In a world where marriages are easier to break than commit to, this one thing is very comforting. There will never come a day when God finds a younger version of me that He would prefer, or one who weighs a little less. He will never seek to find someone who makes fewer mistakes. God loves me (and you) today, exactly the way we are. Of course, that doesn't mean He won't change and grow us. But we can count on the fact that HE will never leave. Never.

Honestly, I think that should be enough, but you know what? God gives us MORE! Not only will he never leave us, look at what Psalm 42:8 says: "*[Yet] the LORD will command his lovingkindness in the daytime, and in the night his song [shall be] with me, [and] my prayer unto the God of my life*" (KJV). I don't know about you, but there have been many sleepless nights around here. What a comfort to know that God gives me His song to be with me in the night and His lovingkindness in the day. This God isn't some being who dictates and controls. He wants a relationship with us. He wants to be that song in the night. What a precious thought!

But there's more. Actually, the Bible is full of verses I could share here, but I will let Psalm 116:1 be enough for today: "*I love the LORD, because he has heard my voice and my pleas for mercy*" (ESV). This isn't the only place in the Bible where it says God hears our cry. In fact, there are far too many to list. But think about it for one second. The God of heaven, who created you in His very image, hears your cry. He knows those lonely thoughts. He sees every tear.

After reading those verses it's hard not to be excited about the promises we have in God. However, I also know those verses can be hard to swallow when they come from a pastor who has been married 20 years and goes to bed every night cuddled with the woman of his dreams. Or from the well-meaning counselor who may have a degree in this stuff, but has never come home to an empty darkness.

I'm not either of those. I still lay on one side of the bed feeling that vast emptiness beside me. I know what it's like to go days without talking to another human, or at least another adult. And I know the anguish of having no one to hold you through life's triumphs and trials. Yes, I understand that God is not in the flesh. And yes, I've heard so many of you say you need someone in the flesh. But, oh my friend, don't you see what you are really saying there? If you need more than what you have, you are saying that God is not enough. **And this thing I can promise: Until God is enough for us, no one else will EVER be enough—no husband, no friend, no family member, no counselor. No one.**

So what does that look like, practically? I mean, if we are to believe these verses and KNOW we are not alone in this, how do we do it? My friend, as I already mentioned, I'm no expert here. But I will tell you what has worked in my life.

1. **Don't allow yourself to speak lies out loud.** Every time you find yourself starting to doubt God or proclaim despair about your situation, stop yourself dead in your tracks. DON'T allow yourself to speak out loud what you are not supposed to believe in your heart. (Don't allow yourself to dwell on it either.) Negative talk will indeed begin to sound true if you continue to say it, so stop right now.

2. **Cling to the truth by drowning in it.** Next, you have to replace those lies with the truth. And if you are anything like me, you don't know nearly enough truth. Carve out that quiet time and DROWN yourself in God's Word until you have a scripture to combat every lie that you think, feel, or say. God tells us His Word is the sword we

Start a notebook!

21

need to fight this battle (Eph. 6). Don't leave your sword on the shelf.

3. **Preach to yourself, I promise this works.** I've been using this tactic for years. I recite verses and truth from God's Word OUT LOUD all the time. I tell my kids what His Word says about something, I put it on my mirrors, and on the fridge. I read it out loud. I cry it out loud. Sometimes I shout it out loud. I even post it on Facebook. This is my chance to be a realist. I allow myself to say, "I FEEL lonely, but I know it's a lie because God commands His lovingkindness over me every day!" This works great when dealing with kids, too. Just remember, as my wise friend always says, "Feelings are real. They just aren't reliable." Feelings aren't taboo. We all feel things, we just can't believe that our feelings are truth. *(http://bit.ly/1pyv6Pm)*

At the risk of contradicting myself, I will share one last thought. Once you find that God is enough, or at least realize you are on a journey to that place of contentment, look around at what God has given you. Maybe there is a single moms group at your church or in your community. I was unable to find one with like-minded gals, so I rely most on online relationships. And I'll be honest, while it seems weird, it's really quite nice. I can talk whenever and not need childcare. There is almost always someone around to talk me down from the ledge. And often times, I find that in helping someone else with their problem, God teaches me something new about my issues.

If you are looking for an online support group, we've got a few. Many overlap with the same people! Not Consumed Single Mom Community *(http://on.fb.me/1ACFXfM)* is a general support group for all single moms. Homeschooling Alone *(http://on.fb. me/10AHaUi)* is support for the single mom who homeschools. Come and join us. We'd love to have you!

Stats and Stories of Other Single Moms

So now you know you aren't alone. But I bet you still hesitate to believe me. I'm guessing this because I've been where you are. I've been in that place where I couldn't imagine that anyone had ever really walked this path. I was certain no one could understand. God had to show me I was believing a lie. So I want to show you, too.

Several years ago, I felt led to start a Facebook group for single moms who were homeschooling. I knew clearly that God was prompting me to do it, but the idea was laughable. I mean, who was going to be in this group? I was certain there couldn't be that many moms in the same situation, but I obeyed anyway. The first week, God showed up in an unbelievable way. Over 100 people joined the group. At the time of the writing of this book, there are over 700 people in this group I was so certain would be empty. Every day, new single moms ask to join and I find myself in awe of God's greatness once again. The moms in the group are doing everything possible to encourage one another on this journey.

I did a survey of those 700+ single homeschooling moms. Before I share with you what they had to say, I want to caution you to remember that God has placed us all in different circumstances. Be careful not to let yourself get discouraged if your situation is different from others, or even different from the norm! It is not a fair comparison.

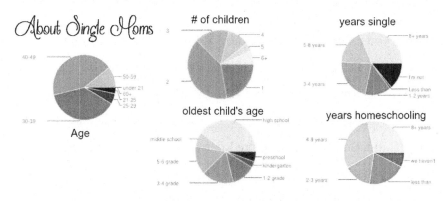

Real, single, homeschool moms said...

I thought I was the only one for many years. I thought it was impossible until I had no choice but to homeschool. Now, I cannot imagine it any other way. God has provided above and beyond what I could have ever imagined. The thought of my son being gone 8-10 hours a day, 5 days a week is way too much. ~Kristie

If a mom feels led to homeschool, then just trust the Lord and follow Him! He will provide everything you need! It won't always be easy, but your children are an eternal investment and your first ministry. He will bless you in ways you could never imagine. ~Jennifer

It IS possible to homeschool. There are other families that might be willing to school your child in specific subjects a couple days a week—to give you "work at home" time. ~Julie

Homeschooling as a single mom is difficult, but not impossible. I thought several times about putting my kids in public school, but didn't really feel comfortable with that decision. Being a single mom, and especially homeschooling as a single mom, is made much easier with some support, whether it comes from family or church. ~Anonymous

My 10 and 11-year-old had such extreme behaviors I was called multiple times a week to school, and I rarely took them into the community because of worries about how they would act/react. Since homeschooling, we frequently go into the community because their behaviors have decreased immensely. ~Tammi

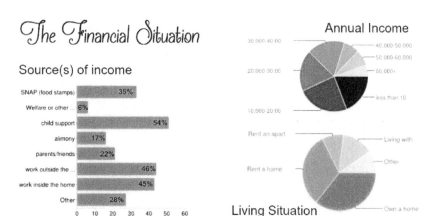

The Financial Situation

Source(s) of income

SNAP (food stamps)	35%
Welfare or other	6%
child support	54%
alimony	17%
parents/friends	22%
work outside the	46%
work inside the home	45%
Other	28%

Annual Income

Living Situation

Real, single, homeschool moms said...

I used to run a full-time business from home. I homeschooled during that time. It is entirely possible for a single parent to work full-time and homeschool. Today, my teens are both succeeding in college. My 16-year-old has been offered university entrance, tuition-free. I don't believe this is an isolated result of homeschooling. People who say single, working parents can't homeschool are problem-focused, not solution-oriented. I say, be a part of the solution, not a part of the problem. ~Anonymous

I worked full-time for a year and realized the toll it was taking on my kids' education and how it increased the stress on our family, so I quit (there were other reasons as well). That year was the first time I had worked so much out of the home since 1988 (I have 7 kids). I decided that I would rather struggle financially (nothing new) than lose my kids just at the end of their homeschooling. We are now in a strange living situation, but I already see a big difference, especially in my 14-year-old. Homeschooling is worth it. ~Laure

This is my last month getting food assistance. I don't like using government programs but I found it necessary while my children were younger. I also just finished college while schooling my children. If you have the desire to homeschool, you can do it. Pray for help and know that you are capable, no matter what others say. ~Anonymous

This was our first year homeschooling and I'm not going to lie and say it was easy. BUT, it was truly an adventure and we found out what works for us. I know what my daughter's strengths and weaknesses are. I have to remind myself not to compare her to others. (I'm the only one out of all my friends who homeschools.) I love my life and all its struggles and glory! I thank God for giving me everything we need. It may not be a lot, but it is ENOUGH! ~Jen

Now I want to share with you the stories of 3 amazing, single homeschool moms. Two have walked this journey far longer than I have. All have a story full of God's amazing grace. So pull up a chair and get a cup of coffee and let's take a peek into their lives. They've each written words of encouragement for you.

Meet Mary Jo

Let's face it: being a single parent intensifies the challenges of homeschooling.

In many two-parent homeschooling families, the dad takes primary responsibility for earning the living and the mom takes primary responsibility for educating the children. The labor is divided and the support is multiplied. Although there are also many two-parent families where both parents contribute to the education and the finances—often through a family business—a single parent is usually solely responsible for both. The labor is multiplied and the support is subtracted.

But the increasing number of single parents choosing to educate their children at home testifies that it can work. Brian Ray of the National Home Education Research Institute says his studies show that about two percent of homeschooling families are headed by single parents, but it is his opinion that this figure probably under-represents the true number.

I have been homeschooling for eight years—four of them as a single mom. The number-one question people ask me (usually with a breathless air of amazement) is, "How do you *do* it all?"

My answer comes in two parts: (1) *I* don't, and (2) I redefine *it all*.

Don't Be a Lone Ranger

None of us—single or married—can homeschool relying on our

own power. But God's grace is sufficient for us, for His strength is made perfect in weakness (2 Corinthians 12:9).

I wouldn't be honest if I didn't confess that some days I really don't know how I can make it. There's just not enough of me to go around. Sometimes I wrestle with exhaustion, discouragement, loneliness, and frustration. I have discovered, though, that the struggle is hardest when I focus on my situation and my inadequacies rather than on the love and providence of God. Turning my eyes to Him helps me remember to "be strong in the Lord and in the power of His might" (Ephesians 6:10, NKJV).

God has indeed proven faithful: "A father of the fatherless, a defender of widows, Is God in His holy habitation" (Psalm 68:5, NKJV). He has provided for all our needs through work I can do at home, help from my parents, supportive friends, and the loving ministry of a godly church.

A support network is helpful for any homeschooler, but particularly crucial for single parents, who lack the help and sounding board of a spouse. Be involved in a local church, and ask folks there to pray for you. Seek out a homeschooling support group in your area. Nurture godly friendships. I frequently consult a few close friends about choices in training and educating my children and seek advice about business matters from fellow Christian entrepreneurs who share my family-based priorities.

You Have Only Twenty-Four Hours in Each Day

Time is your most precious commodity. You can earn more money, but you can never have more than twenty-four hours in a day, so time management is a critical skill for single-parent homeschoolers.

Just as the three most important factors in real estate are Location, Location, Location, the three most important tasks for single parents are Prioritize, Prioritize, Prioritize.

Learn to say no to the good in order to say yes to the best. Limit outside commitments. Too many extracurricular activities can crash a crowded schedule and steal precious family time. You don't have to forego such opportunities entirely; just be intentional and very selective.

Routine tasks such as grocery shopping, going to the bank or post office, and medical appointments can consume far too much time if you're not careful. I've noticed that I feel most overwhelmed when I'm on the go too much. Try to consolidate all errands that require leaving the house into one day a week.

The concept of "opportunity cost" revolutionized my thinking about prioritizing. Every choice you make has a potential opportunity cost. Although this may seem counter-intuitive to frugal homeschoolers, spending an extra hour driving to several different stores to save $5.00 on groceries may not necessarily mean you saved $5.00. If by working that hour you could have earned $20.00, you actually lost $15.00 by "saving" $5.00. I realized that the time I spent running around to yard sales every Saturday morning would be much better used earning income.

Multitasking is one of my top survival secrets. This strategy works well for both parents and children. I start a load of laundry or dust a bookcase when I'm on the phone and pay bills or file papers during teleconferences. I have taught phonics lessons in doctors' waiting rooms, explained basic business concepts in the emergency room, and discussed history and current events in the check-out line at the grocery store. My boys listen to tapes or watch educational videos while they fold laundry. We redeem time in the car by listening to books on tape or reviewing math facts, spelling, or grammar rules.

Make Homeschooling Work

Be realistic in your expectations, particularly about how much time you can devote to direct instruction of your children. It simply may not be possible for your homeschool to match your highest goals, but you can still make it work. My ideal homeschooling scenario would include hours of daily reading aloud to my children, discussing ideas at great length, intensive one-on-one tutoring, and so on, but the necessity of earning a living simply precludes much of that. I relish building my own eclectic educational program from scratch, but it's much more practical for me to use at least some prepared curriculum. I've learned to come up with a realistic educational plan that we can actually implement rather than wasting time fretting over the gap between theory and practice.

It makes sense to teach children together whenever possible. Skills such as math and phonics have to be taught at individual levels, of course, but most subjects can be taught to multiple ages. We usually begin our school time with the whole family coming together for Bible reading, prayer, Scripture memorization, poetry, and classic literature. Then the boys split up for independent work and one-on-one instruction from me.

Children of varying ages can all study the same period of history, same topics in science, etc., with independent assignments at varying levels of difficulty. When we studied American history, for example, we were involved in a weekly co-op where the boys did hands-on activities and presented reports. During the week, Forrest (13) read high school and adult-level history books, Andrew (10) read intermediate-level books, and Andrew also read easier books aloud to Perry (8).

As soon as my children become competent readers, I encourage independent learning. I would prefer a leisurely family-wide read-aloud time for history, for example, but most of the time it's more practical to have the boys read on their own and use our time together to narrate, answer questions, or discuss what they have read.

Learning to take responsibility for their own education teaches children important skills that will be useful in college and adult life. Independent learning also offers the opportunity for each child to pursue his own special interests. Forrest's passions are history and business, Andrew is a scientist and mathematician, and Perry is a talented artist. It's a little early to tell what Thomas (4) will specialize in (demolition work, perhaps?), but he's spending a lot of time these days drawing with Perry.

You can delegate some instruction to older children. I take responsibility for introducing new concepts in math and phonics, for example, but Andrew helps Perry review phonics flashcards, listens to him practice reading aloud, and instructs him on his map work. Perry helps Thomas learn his letters and numbers and teaches him how to draw simple figures.

You can also delegate to technological tutors, but be sure to keep in mind the hazards of too much computer or video time. Forrest and Andrew are currently learning how to type with a computer-based instruction program, and we'll soon be adding computer-based foreign language study. Audiotapes or CDs can be great aids for reviewing math facts, history dates, and so on, and recorded books can supplement live read-aloud time. My boys enjoy listening to Diana Waring's history tapes and Jim Weiss's storytelling tapes as they drift off to sleep each night.

Systematize for Success

Another helpful strategy is to establish systems to make things run smoothly. Some families find that a strict time-based schedule works well. A more flexible approach works better for my family, so I plan more in terms of a routine (things usually happen in a predictable sequence) rather than a schedule (things happen at a certain time).

I have found two systems that work well for my family. Our system for homeschooling involves weekly assignment sheets and an inbox/outbox system. I plan specific daily assignments a week at a time, type them, and print out a list for each child. This helps ensure that the boys know what to do, even if I'm not available. I list all independent lessons, as well as the studies that require my direct instruction or that we'll do as a family, such as Bible, poetry, and reading aloud. The boys check off each lesson as they complete it. (Our rule for schoolwork and chores: it's not finished until it's checked off the list!)

The assignment sheets double as my record-keeping system. Because I type them on the computer, I can make any needed adjustments (sometimes we add or rearrange lessons, and sometimes life intervenes in the best-laid plans), print out a clean copy, and save it in a binder for a permanent record of their work.

We keep stackable trays (available at office supply stores) in our school area, on top of a short bookcase holding current school books, binders, dictionaries, etc. Each child has an inbox where I put his assignment sheet and any papers needed for that week's lessons, such as maps, worksheets, math tests, etc. The boys put their completed work in the top tray, which serves as their outbox and my inbox. After I check their work, I discuss it with them if needed and then transfer the papers to another stack of trays; the boys can then add those pages to their binders or folders.

To deal with the rest of life besides homeschooling, my other system is a chart with an undated four-week grid for each child, listing all daily household chores and personal responsibilities. (I use a simple Excel spreadsheet, but you could draw a basic grid with a pen and ruler.) For example, Andrew's chart includes: make bed before breakfast, brush teeth after breakfast, read Bible, brush teeth after lunch, complete all school assignments, sweep and clean the table after supper, brush teeth before bedtime, clean the litter box or feed cats, put dirty clothes in hamper, put away clean laundry, and drink four glasses of water. These detailed lists, taped to the refrigerator, remind each child of what he needs to do, free me from repeating routine instructions, and allow me to see at a glance what has been done.

My children do nearly all of the housework. I use two principles for assigning chores: divide repetitive tasks and assign work to the youngest child capable. Each of the oldest three boys is responsible for cleaning the table and sweeping the kitchen and dining room after a specific meal, which prevents debate about whose turn it is. When emptying the dishwasher, a taller child puts away glasses and plates into high cabinets, and a shorter child puts away items that belong in drawers and low cabinets. The two middle boys do most of the laundry folding, and the oldest three all put away their own clothes, plus another category of laundry: towels, my clothes, and the youngest's clothes. I usually assign my four-year-old to pick up things from the floor (he's closest to it!). He doesn't have a regular sweeping assignment yet, but I often ask him to use his child-sized broom to sweep up little messes. The oldest two mow and weed-eat the yard after the youngest two pick up sticks and move outdoor toys to clear the way.

Balance Work and Family

The necessity of providing for our families financially, as well as training and educating our children, often presents the biggest challenge to single parents. Just as some two-parent families use creative scheduling (such as evening lessons) to maximize children's time with Dad, single-parent homeschoolers can take advantage of the flexibility of homeschooling to meet their families' unique needs.

Working from home has always been popular with homeschoolers, and this is a particularly good option for single parents. I work at home as a freelance editor, writer, and writing coach. Typically, I concentrate my instructional time with the boys in the mornings and assign them independent lessons, chores, and free time in the afternoons while I work. I also work in the evenings, especially after they go to bed (somehow it's easier to concentrate when the house is quiet). Because my boys visit their father two weekends a month, I reserve that solo time primarily for concentrated work to free up more of my time when they're at home. I also try to schedule a break for myself during their absence: lunch with a friend, a movie, or a couple of hours with a good novel.

Including your children in your work, when possible, is also helpful. Andrew does all my photocopying for a penny a page, and Forrest goes with me to entrepreneurial conferences, where he is learning skills that will help him support a family someday. Depending on their ages, children can learn to design or maintain websites, answer calls from customers, pack and ship orders, take inventory, and many other business tasks.

If your work cannot be done at home, perhaps you can rearrange your schedule to maximize your time at home. A family friend who lost his wife to cancer shifted his work schedule as a piano tuner to two ten-to-twelve-hour days a week so that he can be home with his two young sons most days. He hires homeschool graduates to care for his boys and home on his work days, and his mother and sisters help out occasionally as well. Because he is working more efficiently with this concentrated schedule, he is still earning about 75 percent of his previous full-time income.

Find Time for Fun

Finally, don't neglect to make time for fun as a family. Particularly when you work at home, it is difficult to identify when your "work day" is over. I know just how hard it can be to pull away when deadlines are looming and the electric bill is due, but taking a break is good for you as well as your children, and it can actually make your work time more efficient. My boys know that no matter how busy I am during the week, on Friday night I'm all theirs. "Family Night" is a firm commitment around our home.

God Is Faithful

If God has called you to homeschool your children, He will provide the strength, patience, grace, resources, and time to do it. Let your family and your life be a testimony of God's faithfulness.

Even with all the systems and routines I've described, things don't always go exactly as I've planned. But through God's grace, my children are growing, learning, and flourishing . . . right here at home with me. I wouldn't want it any other way.

Update: A Long-Term Perspective

Nine years have passed since I wrote this article, and I'm still using the strategies I shared in it. They work.

We're beginning our eighteenth year of homeschooling, and

this is my fourteenth year as a single mom. My sons are now 22, 19, 17, and 13, and I'm so proud of the fine young men they have become. The oldest three are Eagle Scouts, and Thomas is well on his way to Eagle. Forrest and Andrew were homeschooled through twelfth grade and are now in college, for which their years of independent learning prepared them well. Forrest is majoring in business, and Andrew is majoring in computer engineering—both of them in fields that their early interests anticipated. They have also taken on the responsibilities of a variety of jobs and entrepreneurial endeavors. I'm still educating Perry (12th grade) and Thomas (8th grade) at home—five more years to go!

If you're in your first few years of homeschooling as a single mom, it may be hard to look past the struggles you encounter every day. I hope that this long-term perspective will encourage you to press on! Remember, although the days can be long and difficult, the years of bringing up your children as a single mom are only a season. As your children grow older, they will become more responsible and independent, which will lighten your burden. Above all, lean on God's mercy, strength, and faithfulness.

Note: Most of this chapter is a reprint of an article I wrote when my sons were 13, 10, 8, and 4; it first appeared in the September/ October 2005 issue of Homeschooling Today. To give you a double perspective from my early years as a single mom with younger children and my current life as a long-time single mom with older kids, I've kept the original article intact and added an encouraging update at the end.

Mary Jo Tate is the author of Flourish: Balance for Homeschool Moms (Apologia) and host of the "Flourish at Home" radio show on the Ultimate Homeschool Radio Network. She is a lifelong bibliophile, an international editor, a speaker, and a time management coach. She blogs at www.FlourishAtHome.com, where she shares encouragement, inspiration, and practical strategies to help moms balance their busy lives.

Meet Columba

A Sacred Ministry

When my husband left, I did not know how divorce would impact my children, then ages four, two, and six months. I didn't know if my ex would be consistent with child support. I didn't know whether to relocate, or stay put. I didn't know how to parent, as 12 years in an abusive church had taught me a strange view of parent-child relationships. Because of the abusive church's teaching, I didn't even know if God still loved my children and me.

But I knew two things:

- My children had lost their dad to divorce.
- They were not going to lose their mom to a job.

I had to do whatever it took to get my kids through the trauma of divorce. They were my sacred ministry.

I thought homeschooling might set a precedent with the courts for my staying home with the kids, which would find its way into my divorce settlement. But I wanted to be sure homeschooling was right for us.

I investigated conventional schooling. In the office of a local school, I watched some telling interactions between a student and the staff.

The boy had broken a rule. He sat, shoulders slumped, clearly embarrassed. The school secretary walked by and mentioned to the boy how wrong his behavior was.

A passing teacher commented on his poor choices.

Another staff member added her two cents; and so it went. Adults demonstrated their discernment and righteous correction—only none of them realized that the last person passing through had already taken care of it.

Poor kid!

The school was likely a fine place in many ways. But discipline was my job. I could not allow my son to be corrected arbitrarily by a dozen staff members who happened by—none of whom could possibly be as invested in his well-being as I was.

Right then, I decided to homeschool.

Other benefits influenced my decision. Even though my faith was shattered by the abusive church, I was on a path of healing. I appreciated the support of Sunday School teachers and pastors, but I believed my children's nurturing in faith was primarily my responsibility. Homeschooling allowed me to pass the knowledge and grace I received on to my children.

I could filter the influences that reached my children, and discuss our culture's messages with them regularly. God would have been with us if I worked outside the home and my children attended conventional school. But homeschooling made it easier to teach them a biblical perspective.

Homeschooling facilitated a healthy lifestyle, too. It gave me better control over our diet and exercise. Poor sleep has been an on-going problem with all my kids. For many months after my husband left, my middle child had nightmares. Had I been forced to awaken my kids early, their schoolwork and perhaps their health may have been compromised.

Finally, homeschooling allowed me to design an education in sync with my children's learning styles and interests. At nine, my oldest son kayaked on the ocean and saw dolphins up close. My second son studied paleontology, and traveled to a dig site in Montana with his dad. My daughter performed in ballets and theater.

A Call to Peace

Depending on my ex financially allowed me to homeschool. I learned to apply Romans 12:18: "If possible, so far as it depends on you, live peaceably with all" (ESV).

Shortly after my ex left, I explained I would not be working until our youngest child turned 18. I didn't know how he would respond to this, or if it would even be possible. But I wanted to take my stand. In the divorce settlement, I stated my beliefs about the need to parent full-time, that it can't be delegated, that I intended to focus on my children throughout their teen years, and that I would not be working until they reached adulthood.

I sweetened the deal by waiving spousal support after raising the kids, promising to diligently seek employment at that time. I spelled it out respectfully, appealing to my ex's reasonable good sense. A church divorce recovery program walked me through detachment, which helped me be business-like and polite.

I was blessed by my ex's agreement to homeschool. Relieving my fears, he was consistent with child and spousal support—a gift I know many single parents can only dream of. He worked hard to keep his financial obligation to the family, and remained involved with the children.

Although money was tight, I learned to budget carefully. I asked only for enough to cover our needs. I was careful to be honest and fair. If a refund came through on something my ex had funded in addition to his regular support, I gave him his share.

The following tips promote peace:

- If your ex is adamantly against homeschooling, be gracious and pray. Respect your ex's perspective, and remember that God is in control.

- Whatever your ex does in support of homeschooling is a blessing. Thank God daily for everything. Also, regularly thank your ex for his contributions.

- Correspond by email rather than in person or by phone. This gives each person a chance to express their thoughts clearly. You can think twice before you hit send. Emails can also be referred to as needed.

- "People with good sense are slow to anger, and it is their glory to overlook an offense" (Proverbs 19:11, CJB). I can't take credit for my ex's supportive decisions, but I could have sabotaged them by stirring up dissension. While serious issues must be addressed, we needn't create an uproar over small matters. Children need stability. Do your part.

Open Hands

For years, I copied homeschool methods that worked for other people, trying to quell massive self-doubt. However, every family is different. I eventually learned to stand by what I knew would work for my unique children. And when I doubted myself, God guided me anyway.

I've used all three of California's legal homeschool options. I began by enrolling my kindergarten son in a private school, as an independent study student. The support of the assigned teacher was wonderful—she had a real gift with children. I had access to some great curriculum, too. I was free to teach my son entirely at home, and the teacher kept our records.

When that program closed, I nervously filed a private school affidavit with the State of California. This option allowed me to use whatever approach I chose. I worried about not having "proper" tests and a traditional learning plan. Subtle criticism from non-homeschoolers intimidated me. Fear cramped my style; but it didn't matter. My children's learning progressed with traditional curriculum.

One evening, I listened to some homeschool moms discuss the state-funded charter school they used, with its funds for supplies and classes and its help with record- keeping. I was excited—and cautious.

Charters have been called a "trojan horse," designed to bring homeschool families back under governmental control. The lure is money for supplies and classes. The sticking point is that Christian curriculum may not be used.

These were huge concerns for me. I didn't want to compromise my mandate to raise my children in the faith. I agreed in principle that the best option is independence from governmental support, with its attached strings. However, money was tight. Prayerfully, I decided to enroll my children.

I chose curriculum that was not hostile to faith. I used the funding for music lessons, classes, and school supplies, and continued to teach my children God's ways. I learned that the heart matters more to God than the form.

When my oldest son approached high school, I reconsidered. By this time, I was more confident in my decisions. I wanted my son free to use a distinctly Christian curriculum; as a teen, he was forming his worldview. In addition, the charter high school program involved bureaucratic red tape. So, I withdrew him from the charter school and again opened my own private school.

I've followed suit with all three of my children. Once they reach high school, they can study what they want, from a Christian perspective.

Our winding homeschool journey illustrates that God guides us, despite our fears and doubts. There's no one right way to homeschool. Discovering what's best for our family is an organic process that unfolds with experience.

Single moms who need help can take it without fear or guilt. Those who can't find a way to make homeschooling work can trust that God is in control, and He is good. The trick is continual openness to change. We do best when we hold our children and our plans up to God, with open hands.

A Sigh of Relief

I've experienced many interruptions and mishaps throughout homeschooling. I've learned to keep the big picture in mind.

Once, we moved to a new house two days before Christmas. The kitchen was torn out. The water ran murky orange for days. My children were sick. I had no cell phone reception, and I couldn't unpack because the flooring wasn't finished.

Many weeks passed before we got back to our schoolwork. While I dealt with the house, my children, then ages four, six, and eight, played endless rounds of Animalopoly and other board games. And they learned their math facts!

When my oldest child was in middle school, I decided I could supplement the child and spousal support by teaching classes that my own children were enrolled in. Because I was now correcting 20 children's work instead of three, our standards dropped. My children's work grew sloppy, and I was too busy to address it. Yet, as I later learned, they were still absorbing an excellent education. And the other benefits of homeschooling were still working in their favor.

In August 2011, my middle child was diagnosed with type 1

diabetes, an incurable autoimmune disease. By October, we were so far behind that I had to switch to a computer-based curriculum, mid-stream. We homeschooled through the following summer to catch up.

Homeschooling works, even when it doesn't. To my surprise and relief, my children have become independent, self-motivated learners despite the interruptions. They can converse intelligently with people of all ages. They're funny and confident.

My oldest son graduated recently. He scored in the 85th percentile on the math section of the SAT, and in the 99th in language arts. He earned top scores on the junior college's admissions tests, placing into their freshman courses at the highest level possible. He knows what he wants, and he breezes through his courses, handling his responsibilities beautifully.

And oh, the bullets we've dodged! Peer pressure and bullying were non-issues. Influential teachers promoting empty, unbiblical beliefs had no access to my children. My children don't see the point of experimenting with drugs and alcohol, or getting into trouble. They have a healthy view of sexuality, intending to continue preserving it for marriage. They're unencumbered with the burdensome issues these conventional school pitfalls present.

My kids aren't being raised in a bubble. They learn from the real world, coming with me to the market, the beach, the museum, the bank—the venues of real life. Access to the Internet exposes them to many beliefs and viewpoints, which we discuss. My oldest son's transition to responsible adulthood has been as simple as swimming from the shallow end to the deep end.

Looking back at 14 years of homeschooling, with a few more to go, I am deeply thankful for God's presence and guidance. I've learned that God is with us, every step of the winding homeschool journey.

Columba Lisa Smith blogs at Single Mom Faith (www.singlemomfaith.com) to encourage single moms to walk strong in their faith. She has homeschooled her three children as single mom throughout their school years.

Meet Latoya

An Unconventional Choice

When I became a mom I didn't know anything about homeschooling. I figured my boys would go to a private school when the time came. I was in law school at the time and figured that I'd easily earn enough money to afford tuition. I was already paying more than my rent in childcare to attend school full-time so I figured it wouldn't be too difficult to simply change the name on the check each month. When my husband moved out I figured that I would just apply for a tuition waiver.

God clearly had other plans. I watched as my oldest really struggled with boredom at the child care center. He was already reading when most of the other children in his class were just starting to learn the alphabet. He also had some sensory and behavioral issues that would have landed him either on meds or in a special program in a classroom.

One day I heard God speak to my heart that I was going to homeschool. I brushed it off for a while because that was just nuts. How in the world was I going to be a lawyer and homeschool my boys on my own? I wasn't. I graduated from law school and started my life as a single stay-at-home mom.

The Importance of Family

I had no idea how my divorce would hurt my boys. They were very young when their dad moved out—almost 1, and 3. I believed that my oldest was used to dad not being around and my youngest wasn't really fully aware of what was going on. I was wrong.

As I struggled to figure out how to be at home and keep food on the table (even spending a few months homeless) I started to see the hurt in my oldest son's heart. He struggled with anger and being sad for reasons he couldn't express. As my little one grew older I noticed that he was hurting as well.

Being home with my boys gave me the gift of being able to help them through this time. We had time to talk and cry, time to heal and grow closer as a family. Over the years at home with my boys we have had some hard times but we have done it as a family. My boys are learning the importance of leaning on God for our needs and wants. And this mama has found new purpose and passion in motherhood.

Homeschooling has also allowed my boys to have more time with dad. Because I set our schedule, it's easy to take a day from school or end early so that my boys can be with their father. Now, he doesn't always take advantage of this but the time is there just the same.

Making it Work

Every homeschooling family is different, and single-parent homes are no exception. My boys are still very young right now so I have dedicated most of my time to teaching and training them. Because of that commitment, I knew that I could not take a job that required me to be away from home. I found that blogging, virtual assistance, and freelance writing have helped me afford to be home with my boys. I'm also in the process of starting a life-coaching business that should help me earn a little more income while still being at home where my heart is.

I have also found that keeping things as simple as I can is a sanity saver. We are not involved in a co-op, my boys don't do sports or extracurricular activities, and I don't spend a ton of money on curriculum. We take advantage of local nature parks, free community events, and are involved in the children's ministries at our local church. This gives me time to teach, work, keep the house running, and still have time for fun and relaxation with my boys.

When it comes to curriculum, we lean toward the Charlotte Mason method. I am able to put together my own curriculum and lessons without breaking the bank. We read lots of great books and use the internet to find fun hands-on activities. I only buy things that I can use with both my boys. Sometimes it's something that we all use together and other times it is something that gets passed down from big brother to little.

Focus on the Blessings

I won't lie and say that it's easy homeschooling as a single mom. I wear many hats and have a lot of responsibility on my shoulders. There are days when the dishes don't get washed and days when the math lessons are skipped completely. One thing that gets me through those tough times is keeping my eyes on God and all the things we are blessed with.

I'm grateful that I get to spend so much time with my boys. It makes it easier when they have to be gone for a while. I love that I can cancel school for a day when the weather is perfect for kite flying or swimming. I get to be there as my boys make new discoveries and master new skills like reading. And I melt into a puddle when my boys tell me that I'm the best teacher/mommy ever.

I never thought that I would be parenting alone. I never thought that I would be homeschooling alone. But I find myself doing both of those things. If you are a single homeschool parent, know that you can do it too. It won't look like a traditional homeschool family (but really, what is that anyway?). It will take some hard work and some creativity, but it can be done. And when God calls you to something, He will also equip you for the job.

LaToya is a single, homeschooling mom of 2 boys. She has a heart and passion for encouraging and equipping women to find their passion and God-given purpose and go after it! She is the author of Beautifully Broken: Finding Joy and Purpose in the Pain. You can find her at www.LaToyaEdwards.net

Getting the Homeschooling Support That You Need

I pray that you have found the stats and stories of so many other homeschooling single moms to be encouragement to your weary soul. I pray that you will reach out to some of us in our little corner of the online world, but I know you will need more support than that. You might physically be the only person in your home who is homeschooling your precious children, but you are certainly not without support. Don't be afraid to go out and find the support you need. It probably won't come knocking down your door, but it isn't as hard to find as you might think.

Family

Maybe you don't have to look far for support. Have you thought much about your family? I know family dynamics can be a tricky thing, but I also know we often fail to communicate our needs effectively. If you have any indication that your family supports you (and I bet there is at least a bit), think through what they might be able to do that would be most helpful to you. Perhaps you have an ongoing or even temporary financial need. Maybe your family could help with the homeschooling. I know many grandparents who homeschool part-time and even some who do it full- time. I even homeschooled my nephew for one year when he was in 2nd grade. Don't hesitate to think outside the box.

My family lives 10 hours away, so they can't be of much help with the day-to-day needs we have. However, we do visit them at least twice a year. During that time, they will often take the kids for a few days so I can catch up on a project or even have a little down time. They also help with clothing needs, since they enjoy doing that. My sister graciously allows me to be on her cell phone bill. Sharing a family plan with her keeps my phone very reasonable.

Church

Since I live so far away from my family, my church family is incredibly vital. If you don't have a church family, finding one should be first on your list of things to do. Look for a church that isn't too small, but isn't too large. You want a place that will take you in and love on your whole family. I've been at two different churches since my divorce. One was the original church our family had attended. It was actually a rather large church (5000 members). I felt at home there and enjoyed the close friendships I had already built. My friends were there to help when I had the baby, they watched my kids several times when I was hospitalized, and even moved girls' night to my house so I could participate when the kids were in bed.

My church now is much smaller (about 1200 members). The kids get great teaching through Sunday school and the Wednesday night program. The nice thing about this church is that the teachers are always the same, so my children are building strong mentor relationships. We also have a very active homeschool group. This is very important to me because this is where my children get their much-needed friendships. This church has helped us moved, donated clothing, food, and other necessities when I was out of work, and provided countless hours of counseling for FREE.

I know there is some hesitation for single moms when it comes to finding a church family. Trust me, when I moved to another state I thought the church- hunting was going to kill me. Be patient. I promise that God will provide if you wait on Him. But there's another little issue we need to address. You will never build a relationship with your church family if you only attend occasionally and never invest. No one will know you and you will find the whole experience to be useless. Go to church often and get involved. Sign up for homeschool events, be a part of a ministry, and introduce yourself to people. It may feel weird or even uncomfortable for you, but God will give you the strength you need to build these crucial relationships. Ask Him to help you! Your church family has a responsibility to support you as much as they can. Let them do it!

Homeschool Community

The homeschool community at large is another great place to find support. We participate in a local co-op that helps me in several ways. First, it is a drop-off program, so it gives me a few hours a week to work. The program teaches Institute for Excellence in Writing (IEW), which is difficult to do at home, plus PE, music, art, and speech. My kids have made so many great friends, which has led to great friendships for our whole family. Yes, I know co-ops often cost money, but don't let that stop you from trying. Perhaps ask your family to pay the fees as part of birthday or Christmas presents. If you need this kind of support, I think you will find the benefits outweigh the cost.

Homeschool Associations and Conventions

When you are looking for support, don't forget homeschool associations and conventions. The HSLDA has an amazing program for single moms. Their website contains great articles and resources to support your journey. In addition, they have a single mom fund which goes to help support single moms who desire to homeschool but need a little more income to do so. *(http://bit.ly/1z87j91)* If you have not applied for this program, go ahead and do it today!

Probably the biggest blessing in my life has been a homeschool convention. When I first started homeschooling, I was already a convention junkie. I've actually been to over 15 conventions in the last 7 or so years. When I walked into Teach Them Diligently Convention, I knew that I had found a home. This convention is like no other. Their focus is missions and discipleship and it shows. Teach Them Diligently has a heart for single moms and has worked hard to create a program that will support and encourage you. You can read more about them on the Not Consumed Blog *(http://bit.ly/1tnI1yo)*.

Challenge 3:
Money

You are still reading, and I'm so glad. It means you are at least entertaining this "crazy" thing of single mom homeschooling. I'm still praying with you, believing that God will meet you right here and give you the encouragement you need to do this!

Hopefully, so far, you've found the motivation to stop listening to those who say it can't be done and found solace for the loneliness. Now we need to a tackle a few practical challenges. These are the things that aren't in our head. They aren't things we can ignore. They are issues we need to face head-on, issues we also need to trust God to help us tackle. First up, money. I know this is the one thing that generally discourages those who desire to homeschool and compels many to throw up their hands in frustration. I don't want this to be you. Is there really a way to make this work? Can you really afford to homeschool as a single mom? Don't be discouraged, my friend, I believe you can find a way! Let's look at some possible sources of income.

Possible Income Sources

1. Child Support and/or Alimony

Of course, the first source of income we think of is child support. This is at least an excellent way to supplement your income, decreasing your own work needs. According to my single mom survey, 54% of homeschooling single moms rely on child support, making it the most popular form of income. We are lucky to live in a time when courts are getting far more strict with child support. Dads are being held accountable for financially supporting their children and free agencies will even help you collect the mandatory child support. Don't be afraid to fight for what you need to take care of your kids. In most states, child support is a set formula. You plug in his salary, yours, number of kids, etc. and it spits out a number. If you are not getting that number, consider contacting your local child support enforcement agency. They will help you for free.

I'm well aware that this amount is generally not enough on which to live. Studies show that divorced women can expect at least a 40% standard of living decrease and this includes the assumption that you are working outside the home. I know from personal experience the difficulty of moving to a smaller house, less affluent neighborhood, and going from brand names to thrift store shopping. But I would encourage you to consider it all meaningless. I'm not saying it was easy, but I quickly learned what is truly valuable in life, which lessened the pressure monetarily. We will talk about ways to save money and cut costs later, but for now I would challenge you with this thought: The lower your cost of living, the less you will have to work, which of course translates into more smiles, hugs, and giggles from those sweet kids of yours.

2. Outside Support

There are many ways to get outside support for your homeschool journey. Nearly 14% of the single moms polled in my survey are living with family or friends. This is an excellent way to cut your expenses so you can homeschool. I know the idea of moving in with your parents likely doesn't sound appealing for most, but for a season, it could allow you time to work on a business plan, build up some income, or even earn a needed certification/degree.

Another source of outside support is homeschool agencies such as the HSLDA. These agencies have resources for single moms, including scholarship funds. Don't be afraid to seek these out and apply. You never know if this is the way through which God will provide for your family.

3. Government Assistance

This is always a sticky subject. As Americans, our country was founded on the principles of hard work and sacrifice. Not many people are in favor of the way government assistance programs look today, as so many abuse the system. Forget all of that. You are not that person. And it doesn't matter what other people think anyway. Government assistance was created for people in times of need. At least at the beginning, you may need to rely on these programs for help. You might be interested in hearing that 35% of the single moms surveyed were using SNAP (formerly food stamps) services.

If you find that you need to use this service, don't be ashamed. Some reports show that nearly 20% of our society (which includes 2-parent homes) uses SNAP to supplement their food costs. I know for me personally, those first few years would have been impossible without it. I don't know if I would have had the resources to create my business and grow it to sustainability without SNAP. Now my family doesn't need that assistance and someone else can benefit the way we did when times were the toughest.

Practically speaking, you can apply for SNAP at your local department of social services office; Google will help you find the information. Each state has different requirements, but most have an online application process which is rather helpful for single moms. The process can take 30-60 days depending on the state, so don't wait until your pantry is completely empty before you explore this option.

4. Employment

Single moms who desire to homeschool need to think outside the box when it comes to jobs. Most of us need one, but it doesn't have to look the way it used to. Some moms work nights or off-hours outside the home and pay babysitters. Some rely on family members to help with childcare and/or the actual homeschooling. Many others work from home. Don't be afraid to look into something that is totally unknown to you. There is a multitude of resources on the web to help you. In fact, Real Ways to Earn Money Online *(http://bit.ly/10AHH8E)* is an entire site devoted to this topic. A popular site for locating jobs is Rat Race Rebellion *(http://bit.ly/1mOLKEO)*. I also enjoyed this article on Real Jobs for Stay At Home Moms *(http://bit.ly/1uID3mn)*. I keep track of all the ideas I run across on my Work at Home Mom Pinterest board *(http://bit.ly/113N7u3)*.

Some questions to think about as you explore the possibilities for you: What are your skills and how might you use those at home instead of in a traditional setting? Is there something you are qualified to do, but have never pursued? What is your passion?

Is there one thing that people are always saying you do well? If so, how can you use that talent to make money?

When I polled our single mom homeschooling group, I was completely amazed at the options and creativity out there. I would say that the two most popular options were working for a call center in customer service, and running a home daycare. There were also quite a few people running their own business from home. The group was split about 50/50 in regard to working from home and working outside the home. Many of those who indicated that they work outside the home were working in the medical field on night/weekend shift. Based on the survey, here is a further list to get you thinking:

- teaching nights at the university
- blogging, virtual assisting, social media work
- tax preparation in home
- licensed in-home child care
- private speech therapy in home
- professional organizing business
- direct sales such as Tupperware
- writing, ghost writing
- web design
- party planning
- tutoring
- creating and selling products (etsy, ebay)

- freelance editing
- massage therapy
- housekeeping for others
- music lessons
- newpaper carrier
- bookkeeping
- nurse or medical caregiver
- dog groomer
- retail sales
- customer service/call center rep

Now that you know there's a myriad of opportunities available, let me share in detail what I have done and how you could do it too.

What I do to bring in money

I remember very clearly the day I knew God wanted me to start a blog. And I'll be honest, I thought He was nuts.

The storm had been raging in my home for over a year and it seemed that despite any attempts or desires on my part, my husband was going to file for a divorce. *(http://bit.ly/13TYVjy)* This blog thing was the answer to a prayer I had been praying for nearly a year: **"Lord, what am I going to do now?"** Although I had a master's degree in teaching, I hadn't worked in 10 years. I had 4 children under 6, one of whom was just a few months old.

I couldn't even dream of going back to teaching. It wouldn't even have paid for the childcare. Not to mention, my 2 school-aged children had only been homeschooled and there was already enough transition in our home. I didn't want to add to the fire.

So, I had to choose to believe that God would indeed provide for us through this entity called a blog. The funny thing was, I knew almost nothing about blogs. I had followed a few on homeschooling and family life. I even had my own little Blogspot blog where I shared pictures with my granny and the rest of my out-of-town family. But the idea of CREATING a blog was foreign. I mean, I felt like I was doing well most days to check email and figure out Facebook.

I had serious doubts that you could even make money with a blog. Sure, I had heard it was so, but I guess I couldn't fathom it. Blogging and/or any type of internet business is still a new enough concept that most people can't quite grasp what it is. In fact, when I tell people I'm a blogger, it's not uncommon to hear, "But what's your real job?" Well, this is my real job now. It took me long enough to accept God's idea of my real job, but I'm so glad I did.

Can I Make Money Blogging?

The simple answer is yes, you can make money blogging. Yes, you can make a lot of money blogging. And, yes, you can even make a full-time income that supports your family. In fact, there are thousands of people who do it. But there are 2 things you need to know before you run out and start your own blog.

First, making money blogging is very hard work. Don't imagine popping on the internet a few hours a week and reaping the benefits of a fat bank account. In fact, you probably won't make anything if you only give it a few hours a week. Blogging is a business, and as with any business, it's going to take a lot of work to start it. Eventually, you might find it running more smoothly. But in the beginning, don't be surprised if you are like one of the many bloggers who work 40+ hours a week. (I've actually clocked 60+ on many occasions.) Think entrepreneur here.

The good news is, you can work those hours whenever it is best for you. When my kids are gone, I work like a dog. There are some Saturdays that I don't even shower. I literally work from 6am until 11pm. I prefer to work hard on those days so I can spend quality time with my kids when they are here. Most of the time I work early mornings and late nights, with some afternoon time thrown in there. You can see my specific schedule here *(http://bit.ly/1tnIznV)*. But again, the point is that I get to choose WHEN I work.

Second, making money blogging is going to cost you. This is the biggest mistake I see people make. They want to start a blog, but they have no money to put into it. I know this is a big mistake because I am guilty of it. I promise you this, if you want to make money, you will need to invest money. It's a very simple and well-known business practice. Have you ever met a restaurant owner who packed out his restaurant before he opened the doors? Of course not. He had to invest in the building, hiring, and planning before he could reap the benefits of that business. I'm not saying that you need $20,000 to start a blog. It's certainly a whole lot cheaper than a brick and mortar business, but you will need to invest in hosting, a domain name, some excellent training, and possibly even some coaching. Plus, you will want to consider blogging conferences, as well as other expenses rather quickly. Once I started investing in high quality training, email providers, and things like that, I actually started making money. I really wish I had known that up front! I could have been making money right from the start.

How exactly do bloggers make money?

There are 4 main ways that bloggers make money: banner ads, affiliate sales, sponsored content, and product sales.

I know plenty of bloggers who feed their family entirely through those little **banner ads** you see on their sites. So the next time you feel a little annoyed by an ad, try to remember that just by looking at that ad, you are helping someone feed their family.

Next on the list is **affiliate sales**. This is money a blogger makes when she shares someone else's product with her readers. Think of it like the old Sears appliance salesman. If you buy a product that a blogger recommends, she will get a small commission from the creator of the product. This is usually how a newer blogger gets started making money. Almost every company has an affiliate program, from Amazon to Gymboree.

Sponsored content is a little harder to explain. This might be a post that a company has funded or from an email campaign. You will see a little note at the bottom of the post when the content is sponsored. It DOESN'T mean that someone has paid the blogger to write nice things. (We get to share our honest opinions, thankfully!) It simply means that the blogger was paid to advertise for that company. Most bloggers choose the companies they will work with very carefully. I know I certainly do. I want to make sure it is consistent with my message and that my readers will benefit.

Finally, bloggers make money through product sales. You probably know exactly what I mean by products. They are those cute little things we create to sell to you! Like my Bible study on obedience *(http://bit.ly/1x9Xyt8)* or these life-saving Breakfast Station packs *(http://bit.ly/1uIDxZR)* that are making everyone's morning so much easier.

Should I Start a Blog?

So now that you understand a little bit about this blogging thing, the next question you might ask is: Should I start a blog? Blogging is indeed a fantastic way to make money, but this answer isn't quite so simple. I'll tell you this, not everyone who starts a blog is successful. In fact, there is something crazy like a 76% fail rate. I think this happens for 3 main reasons:

1. It wasn't God's plan to begin with.
2. The blogger tried to mimic others instead of being their own best awesome.
3. The blogger didn't invest time and money to get started.

So, my advice to you would first be to take this matter to God. If God is leading you to start a blog, then take that leap of faith and obey. If you aren't so sure yet, wait on Him to guide you! Next, spend some money investing in the resources you need to get started the RIGHT way! Then, start making a massive list of all those things you LOVE to talk about. What makes you who you are? What are you passionate about?

Are you interested in this line of work, but simply cannot invest much time or money? **There are other options for you.** I would suggest that rather than starting your own blog, you consider working as a virtual assistant, doing graphic design, running social media, or even writing posts for bloggers. You'll need to work hard to get your name out there, but then you can work as it suits you.

I offer coaching services to single moms who are interested in learning more about starting an online business, either as a blogger or one of the other options mentioned above. If you are interested in pursuing this and wish to have some guidance, please email me at kim@notconsumed.com! This is not a free service, as I have to feed my family and be sensitive with their time. However, I offer this ONLY for single moms as a ministry and feel that it is very reasonably priced with that mission in mind.

Creative Cost Cutting

I'm fairly sure you know the saying, "A penny saved is a penny earned." There are lots of practical ways to save money in order to survive on a very limited income. There's no question that homeschooling as a single mom can be a drastic sacrifice, but most of us would say that giving up those new jeans or trendy haircuts will reap amazing benefits in the hearts of our kids. The entire list of ways to cut costs could never be covered here, but how about a few ideas to get you started?

Share

By far, one of the most common things I hear from single moms who homeschool is that they live with their parents. What a blessing to be able to split the cost of living! Perhaps this is an option for you. If not, there are plenty of other things you can share. As I mentioned earlier, my sister and I share a cell phone bill. We get great rates on a family plan this way. Another option might be to share a membership to a discount club such as Costco.

You can name one other member on your card and it is ok if that member doesn't live in your home. As with anything, please be sure you check the terms of service.

Train Yourself to Be a Savvy Shopper

I know that finding good deals is sometimes easier said than done. I also know that time is short. Just remember, sometimes we need to invest time or money into something on the front end so things will be better in the long run. Couponing is one of those things. It takes time to learn the system. There is no escaping this fact, but once you learn, you won't forget and you can live a lifetime with smarter shopping habits. This is something I had to specifically train myself in. My single momma bought what she could afford when she could afford it. As a result, she spent more money and I learned some pretty bad habits when it came to spending. I've retrained myself and even got to the point where I was able to feed a family of 5 on $200 a month. You can do it too! Learn about couponing here: *http://bit.ly/1lo5AHV*. Try subscribing to blogs that specialize in teaching you how to live frugally, such as *Money Saving Mom* ® (*http://bit.ly/1u88aX2*). Another trick is to read posts and ideas from other frugal people. We all have amazing advice and ideas to share with one another. I keep a frugal living Pinterest board here: *http://bit.ly/1GzqBsV*.

You Need a Budget

I hope I don't need to convince you that keeping a budget is the best way to save more, spend less, and assure your financial health. Just as learning to coupon or shop frugally takes time, budgeting will demand that you dedicate some time to it. I promise it is worth it. It's tempting as a single mom to say that you have no money coming in and you just need to be as absolutely frugal as possible. That is not enough. You still buy groceries and you still need a plan. Get some good budgeting advice from a trusted expert, such as Dave Ramsey, then make a budget you can stick to! The Beginner's Guide to Savings is a great place to start *(http:// bit.ly/1zBB8Su)*.

Book

Identify your largest negotiable expense and find ways to cut it

I imagine that your largest expense is housing or utilities. It's possible that those things are negotiable, but it's also possible that they are not. For me, I spend way more on rent than I want. However, child custody laws require me to have separate bedrooms for my boys and girls, so I rent a 3-bedroom house. The only way I can negotiate this expense is to buy a house, which I plan to do eventually. In the short term, there are many other ways to cut costs, and these are truly negotiable. One example would be homeschooling materials. Look for free or inexpensive

73

ways to obtain homeschool materials. Free Homeschool Deals is one of many sites with ideas *(http://bit.ly/10AIUwD)*. If you aren't following this site, start today. My friend Jamerrill is mom to 8 kids and they live on a single income. She is married, but her advice is still very relevant to us. Also, many states have programs or scholarships for homeschool materials.

Get comfy with the world of second hand

A good thrift store can be any single mom's best friend! The trick is to go often and buy things ahead. So what if Junior isn't wearing size 6 yet. He is going to grow, right? My local thrift store frequently has half-off on kids clothes. The sales are unannounced, but always on Saturdays, so I try my best to hop in there as many Saturdays as I can. You can ask the employees at your store if they run specials and how you can find out about them. Last fall, I bought an entire soccer uniform (minus the team shirt) at our thrift store for $5, shoes included. Saving money in places like this enables me to pay the fee to sign him up for soccer to begin with. We'll talk more about clothing a little later.

Also, don't forget to sell your stuff. If you are done with something, sell it; there is no reason to keep it lying around. Ebay or craigslist are great options. Also, many towns now have local garage sale type groups on Facebook. Do a search and see what comes up for your area. I have learned to keep material possessions lean. I've kept a roof over our heads for quite some time by selling the things that once seemed necessary, but now seem irrelevant. (We even sold our only TV a few years ago!)

Learn to DIY

It's no secret that you save money when you do things yourself. But there is an underlying assumption that DIY is something busy moms simply cannot do. I know because I USED to believe that notion. It's easy to be convinced that you simply don't have the skills, time, or even the motivation to DIY. The truth is, initially it does take a little extra time to plan and put things together, but once you've laid the groundwork, the benefits are so amazing you'll find yourself wondering why you waited so long to do it!

You'll find health benefits such as being able to cut out or limit high fructose corn syrup, or the comfort of knowing the bug spray you use isn't toxic to your small children. Of course, there is also the most motivating of benefits: saving money. With a simple task like making your own laundry detergent, you can save your family up to $400 a year. Since it takes me about 10 minutes to make a year's worth of laundry soap, I think that is a fair trade! Here are 5 areas in which to consider cost-cutting DIY alternatives:

1. Convenience Food

As a single mom, I know exactly how nice those little prepackaged foods are. They're just grab-and-go. But that grabbing is costly both for the waistline and the pocketbook. You can totally do this yourself. Let's take chips or pretzels for example. Why buy individually packaged items? Enlist the kiddos and make up snack bags with your own zip-top bags (that you buy with a coupon on sale). Then the next time you need a fast snack, you've got them ready. I generally store stuff like this in plastic shoeboxes or baskets in our pantry.

When my grocery budget was drastically slashed, I started with the little things like packaged foods. I made all of my own mixes—everything from pancakes to taco seasoning *(http://bit.ly/1iqL33Q)*. It drastically cut the cost and the chemicals! Now I am also a firm believer in bulk cooking and spending a few hours each month stocking my freezer with meals such as these freezer meal plans from Costco and Sam's *(http://bit.ly/1otXvW3)*. And of course, easy DIY breakfasts are always ready at my house with the Breakfast Station *(http://bit.ly/1uIDxZR)*.

2. Haircuts

I know this one seems scary unless you went to cosmetology school, but trust me, you can do it. I was terrified at first. The key is to have the right tools. Here is a great video to get you started with the little boys: *http://bit.ly/13U0w9b*. I actually just totally buzz-cut both of my boys because I love how cute they look. It's also super simple. My boys need cuts every 4-6 weeks, so this saves me at least $400 a year.

You can also trim up your girls with this video: *http://bit.ly/1pyyeuy.* In the interest of honesty, I'll share that I don't usually cut my girls' hair. I have done it in the past and it's simple. However, they only need a trim once a year, so I enjoy making a big deal out of it and taking them to the salon for a girls' day. (Side note: I get my hair cut that day, too.)

3. Cleaning supplies

This is one I wish I had started 10 years ago. Oh the savings I missed out on! Homemade cleaners are easy to make and you really don't need very many. In fact, I only make 3 and they clean my entire house. I can make all 3 in less than an hour from start to clean up and they last me 6 months to a year (depending on the item)!

I started with laundry soap. I like this powder recipe: *http://bit.ly/1Eq4weo.* It's so crazy-easy. I'd also like to try my friend Jamerrill's recipe for liquid laundry soap: *http://bit.ly/1xjhA33.* My powder works fine for us, but if you need strong stain remover, I'd definitely go with the liquid. Jamerrill's hubby works on cars and she can get his clothes clean, so you know it works!

Laundry soap was so freeing and frugal that I also branched out to dish soap *(http://bit.ly/1oMaPS5)* and an all-purpose cleaner *(http://bit.ly/1rXwzfo).*

77

4. Cosmetics

I'm not big on cosmetics per se, but we do have some needs and those things can get rather expensive. I first tried making the shaving cream *(http://bit.ly/1wDf0oo)*, but I also love to make dry shampoo *(http://bit.ly/1lTcTIS)*, bug spray *(http://bit.ly/1uJNozj)*, sunscreen *(http://bit.ly/1m97RaL)*, and anti-itch salve *(http://bit. ly/1tKhaAm)*. I would suggest thinking about the products you spend the most on and then searching Pinterest for a recipe that might work for you. Little by little you can make the transition.

5. Gifts

Whether it's Christmas or birthdays, gift-giving can be costly. Even if you don't consider yourself crafty, there are tons of great ideas out there for you. My favorite resource for this is a series my friend Toni did over at *The Happy Housewife (http:// bit.ly/1tS3LaR)*. She shares 100+ DIY Christmas gift ideas that you really could use any time of the year. I've also got a Pinterest board with ideas *(http://bit.ly/1zBC5u4)*.

Affording Food For Your Family

Let's face it, food comes first for the majority of us when we think about our most basic of needs. Food is something that must be tackled at least 3 times a day, every day, and if you are a single mom, food is likely your biggest struggle. There is not one ounce of judgement here, my friend. I know all too well how easy it is to become a familiar face at the nearest drive-thru. Most single moms are balancing a full-time job, full-time parenting without help, homeschooling or homework help, and about 1000 other things. The schedule is certainly busy, but we don't have to resort to those golden arches. I promise there are simple, frugal, and manageable options out there! So let's take a look at some frugal and simple food solutions!

Shop Smart

Why spend more on groceries when that money could go to rent, electricity, or even something fun? We've already talked some about couponing, but I wanted to share a specific method. I use the Favado app *(http://bit.ly/1pyApOI)* to help me find the sales at each of my key stores (more on this below). The app even tells me if there is a coupon. I select the coupon and then make my list right in the app. It's beautiful! Also, if you are new to using coupons or want to learn more, check out Jenni at Southern Savers *(http://bit.ly/1pyAsdx)*. She has tons of helpful videos and information.

I shop at 3 key stores: Publix, Aldi, and Costco, but I don't shop at all 3 each week. In fact, sometimes I don't even *shop* every week! Once you establish a regular plan, you will find that is not necessary. Here is what I use each store for: Publix (weekly): stockpile from the sales with coupons, produce, meat; Aldi or

Walmart (weekly): produce, dairy, staples; Costco (monthly): flax, quinoa, gluten-free snacks, etc. (Meat and dairy are NEVER cheaper at Costco!)

Use the resources:
WIC, Food Stamps, Food bank

As we've already established, food stamps are not just for the homeless. In fact, a large part of our society uses them. Most single moms simply do not get enough child support (if any) to pay all the bills. Friends, don't be quick to heap shame upon yourself for using government services when times are tough. That is indeed why they are there. If you qualify for WIC or food stamps, use them. Single parenting is hard enough; there is no reason to worry about what someone might think. In the 4.5 years since I've been a single mom, we've used the food bank, WIC, and food stamps. God has provided in bigger ways than these resources could ever promise, but I'm thankful we had them when we most needed them.

Eat Cheap

This is probably an obvious one, but I figured I'd throw out a few of my favorite cheap-eats tips. I use a lot of resources to help me with this since we are gluten free. A simple resource for gluten free meals that are fast and cheap is 31 Days of Gluten Free Meals (*http://bit.ly/1uJOn2i*). A few other things I do:

- **Skip the meat:** trade it for beans, quinoa, or an egg-based dish.
- **Use fillers:** when we do eat meat, I use it sparingly and fill in the meal with pasta or rice.
- **Avoid packages:** as a general rule, if it comes in a package, it costs more and is less healthy. A 5 lb bag of potatoes will go a lot further than a box or two of 99 cent au gratin potatoes.
- **Leftover night:** institute a leftover night once a week. This will clean out the fridge and save on the cost of yet another meal.

Once you've tackled the grocery store, there is still much to do to actually get dinner on the table. Believe me, I know that food preparation can be daunting, but it doesn't have to be. I'm going to suggest several different ways to tackle the food prep. I've done them all and I'll say this: all of them will work to save time. Find one that works well for you, or use a combination of the best ones. There is no right or wrong here.

Bulk Cook

The concept behind this is simple. In fact, I did it tonight. I made 2 batches of sautéed okra *(http://bit.ly/1ygmcoP)*. One was for dinner and the other will go for dinner later this week. This concept works great for spaghetti sauce, baked chicken, browned ground beef, soup, etc. I always think ahead. I never boil 3-4 eggs,

I boil a dozen. I never make one batch of breakfast muffins, I bake 2-3 batches and freeze the rest. I think you get the idea.

Weekly/Monthly Prep

This idea is genius: Spend a few hours in the kitchen and be done for the week, month, or maybe more! These weekly prep ideas *(http://bit.ly/1xjjfW7)* helped me to streamline the fruit and fresh veggies that we have in our house, but I needed more. In an effort to rescue my kids from sugary cereal and Pop-Tarts, I developed a breakfast station that promises 2+ months of DIY breakfasts for the little ones *(http://bit.ly/1uIDxZR)*. This is a life saver for me. I only need to be involved once every few months and then the kids make breakfast on their own!

The good news is, you don't have to reserve this kind of cooking for breakfast only. I have a lunch pack here and many of my friends have great dinner packs for you *(http://bit.ly/1xjjfW7)*. Check out this freezer to crockpot pack and the packs at $5 Dinners *(http://bit.ly/1uJOn2i)*. These plans offer you complete shopping lists, recipes, labels, and more. You can't beat that!

Meal Themes

Perhaps one of my favorite ideas ever is to have weekly themes for your meals. This can be done one of two ways. First, you can have a theme for the whole week. My favorite is Black Beans *(http://bit.ly/1Eq5yXR)*. Yes, you can absolutely make 5-7 original meals with one main ingredient and you will save a ton of money and time while doing it. The second method is to have a theme for each night. The theme reoccurs each week. It would look something like this:

Monday: pasta

Tuesday: chicken

Wednesday: soup and salad

Thursday: beans

Friday: pizza

Saturday: beef or turkey

Sunday: leftovers

You get the idea. Each week you can get creative as to how you will fill the theme. Maybe you have tacos on one Saturday night and roast the next. Of course, there's hamburgers, too. It's so fun to think about food in a different way! You could even get the kids involved with this. Whatever you do, don't let yourself get overwhelmed with the food issue. There are plenty of practical ways to make it a pleasant experience in your home!

Affording Clothes for Your Family

For most families, clothing can be a huge source of stress. Whether it's affording to buy clothes, finding something modest, or figuring out how to store things, kids clothing is a challenge. But, it doesn't have to be. Let's embark together on "Operation Kids Clothes" for a frugal and organized way to manage all your clothing.

1. Buy it

I don't pay for kids clothes. In fact, I've been clothing my kids for FREE for years now. How do I do it? I don't pay more for the clothing than I can resell that same clothing for. Here's what I mean: I shop bargain places for the clothes we wear and I generally buy only high-quality clothing. By sticking to high-quality clothes, I ensure that there is a good chance the clothing will make it through my kids and still be in reasonable condition for me to resell it. My price point on most things is $1, but I am willing to splurge and pay $2-3 for coats and dress clothes.

Where to buy

- **Yard Sales:** Don't knock it until you try it. Yes, it takes time, but if you do it right, you will only need about 1 hour on a Saturday morning. I get amazing deals at yard sales. In fact, sometimes people want to get rid of their clothes so badly that they give me the entire bin for a very low cost. If you are looking for a specific size, I would suggest seeking out yard sales that are advertising those sizes. You can even call or email if they have advertised on craigslist and ask them what sizes they have. I usually skip this part since I have 4 kids. If it says kids clothes in the ad, it's worth stopping by.

- **Consignment Sales:** I used to live in an amazing community with 30 or so churches that had consignment sales each fall and spring. I would go on the half-price day and often find all kinds of gems! Note, this is not a consignment store, this is a short-term sale that usually runs through the weekend. Google the terms "consignment sale" and your city's name to see if there is anything local.

- **Online Sites:** Often people will have large lots of clothes on Ebay or list them on craigslist. This can be a great way to get super-cheap clothes. I've also seen Facebook groups cropping up with "local sales" groups. These can be great for scoring clothes and other items locally.

- **Thrift Stores:** As a last resort I hit up our local thrift store or Goodwill. Typically, they want more for their clothes than I am willing to pay; however, they do run sales when they have a surplus of clothing. You just have to check back often to hit these deals.

- **Friends:** Don't forget the power of friends. Perhaps you can start a clothing swap with your friends, or ask a friend who is done with a size if you can buy it from her. Chances are, she will give you a fair price and be happy to have it off her hands.

- **Stores:** I hardly ever buy clothing at a traditional store, but it's worth mentioning two favorites when it comes to finding something specific you need, or if you simply can't find the time to go to the above-mentioned places. If I have to shop in a store, it will be Children's Place or Kohl's. Both have outstanding customer perks and coupons. If you shop with their coupons, you can get a lot of clothing for next-to-nothing.

The secret key

To keep myself from needing to constantly pop into every thrift store or hit every single garage sale, I stock up. I buy at least two sizes ahead of what my kids are currently wearing, that way I can make sure I have enough when they get to that size. After a shopping trip, I usually make notes in my phone (I use Evernote) as to what I bought for a particular size. This way I don't end up with 30 t-shirts and no shorts. I also buy clothes (in stores) when they are on clearance. Yep, that means I buy shorts in the winter. I also buy enough socks for the whole year during back-to-school sales. They are always super-cheap then.

Reselling the clothes

I prefer the yard sale method for reselling clothes. It's just easier than tagging the clothes for a consignment sale (although I've done that and made very good money doing so). You could also put them up in a big lot on craigslist or that Facebook group you found. Someone will come along and snag them up. Again, I sell my stuff for the same price I paid for it (mostly $1). I have no trouble getting rid of it that way, and let's face it, after going through at least 3 kids, it's probably not worth much more than that anyway!

2. Organize it for now

So now that you have all these clothes, what are you going to do with them? I've found a few very helpful ideas for making this task less overwhelming. One is that I am not picky about how my kids put their clothes away. I do teach them the best way, but the truth is, it doesn't matter if the pants are on the right side of the drawer. I'd much rather let them put their own clothes away than fight that kind of battle. That being said, here are a few other ideas:

- **Socks:** I buy only white socks. I know, such a boring mom, but this way no one spends hours trying to match up socks. All they need to match up is size. I make this easy too, by purchasing a different brand of sock for each family member. Then, the socks just need to be sorted by family member and put away. This one tip has probably saved me 3-4 years of my life.

- **Neutral Bottoms:** I started this when my kids were little, and it was so they would pretty much always match. Everything goes with jeans or khakis. There is no need for a war over mismatched colors when you are getting ready to go to Aunt Bertha's house for a nice dinner. If the bottoms are neutral, any top will probably work!

- **Throw out the dressers:** Seems like a crazy idea, I know. But I much prefer to use boxes or bins for clothing—one bin for shirts, one for pants. It really is far easier than trying to organize tiny drawers that all come unraveled when your child takes his favorite shirt from the bottom of the stack. My little guy uses one of those cube units from Target and the cloth bins inside. As kids get older, it can be tricky getting clothes in here, though. I use larger bins for the big kids. I buy these on clearance at Hobby Lobby, Michaels, Walmart, Target, etc. Whenever I'm in there, I just peek to see what they have. You could also use bins from the Dollar Store.

- **Family Closet:** This is the best idea I know for organizing your family's clothes. Simply find a space where everyone's clothes are stored. This simplifies the laundry process and the dirty clothes issue. It also could provide a place to store future sizes, if you have room. You can find a few ideas here *(http://bit.ly/1xtZqLQ)* or here *(http:// bit.ly/1xH6GSY)*. A quick search of Pinterest will land you tons of links for ideas. One day, I will set this up. For now,

I simply don't have space to do it.

3. Store it for later

If I am buying in advance, I just throw the clothes in a large bin and label it accordingly. If one kid has worn the size, but another will wear it later, I pack it away in the same manner. I actually store my bins in the garage, lined up on the wall. This keeps them accessible when I buy new things. I sometimes put them up in the attic if the time frame is far away. This is especially helpful with clothes that an older child wears but the younger won't wear for 2+ years.

Challenge 4:

Setting up Your Homeschool

Now we come to the homeschooling part of "single mom homeschooling." However, before we can even get started setting up your homeschool, we are going to need to tackle two things if you don't want your life to be miserable. First, let's remember that you are not that goat-owning, 15-passenger van driving, married homeschool mom we talked about in the beginning of this book. So don't try to be like her. If you try to model your homeschool exactly like your married friend's homeschool, you may find failure around the corner. Remember to embrace your differences. Remember that you have different needs than she does. It's great to get ideas from others, but don't do it if you are tempted to forget your own unique needs.

The second thing to remember is that you are not running a branch of the public school, so don't try to make it look like one. This is something that so many homeschoolers are guilty of. In fact, I was one of those people for the first few years. We get all caught up in the "need" for little school desks, workbooks for every subject, a dedicated school space, and 8 hours of school a day. Don't fall for that. Remember, there is a reason you aren't sending your kids to school. Why try and copy the place you are avoiding? Trust me, none of those things are necessary for raising strong lifelong learners!

With that being said, how about a little tour? I don't know about you, but I think it is fun to take a peek around my friends' homeschools. There are so many ideas to share! The cool thing about learning is that we are all CONSTANTLY a work in progress. Sometimes a better idea comes along and we throw out something awesome that we have always done to accommodate this new idea. Sometimes circumstances change and we find ourselves learning new things. It is with great humility that I share with you my simple homeschool. From the pencils to the curriculum, this is the stuff that works in my single-mama home. **So come on inside and let me show you around!**

The physical set-up

It all starts with a good place to make it happen, right? I've told the Tale of My Two Schoolrooms *(http://bit.ly/1tS59u6)* before and how I came to the conclusion that having school in the place we live is most effective for my family. It was hard for this former classroom teacher who REALLY wanted cute little desks with alphabet strips and pencil boxes. But life happens and school can't really be separated for us, so we have grown into our latest set-up: The Practical and Simple Homeschool Room *(http://bit.ly/1pyBqGI)*. With this set-up, school happens right at the kitchen table. All the supplies are there AND I can chop carrots for dinner while calling out spelling words. It's a lifesaver for me.

Simple Homeschool Supplies

Of course, there is more to organizing your space than just figuring out where the bodies will sit. You are going to need some supplies! The Practical and Simple Homeschool room includes a detailed look at how I presently organize all our supplies. Wondering what to buy? I like to stock up during back-to-school sales on the annual stuff, and of course there are some one-time purchases as well.

One-time purchase supplies

- **ipad** *(http://amzn.to/1EcAdG1)*–Yes, I find this incredibly helpful. See how we use apps in our homeschool. *(http://bit.ly/1zfm2j3)*

- **Printer**—I have two printers that I honestly think are the absolute best. I use a Brother color printer *(http://amzn. to/1uIHH3W)* and a Black and White laser printer *(http:// amzn.to/1tnNl4W)*. Why two? Well, the color printer allows me to print those fun printables that just aren't the same without color. Because it's a Brother, the ink cartridges are super cheap AND you can even get generic ones. I've saved tons of money on this printer. But, I do print a lot of stuff that doesn't need to be in color (like coupons and most of our homeschool stuff). That's where the black and white laser printer comes in. This guy is a workhorse. Because it works with toner and not cartridges, I can print as many as 2500 pages on one toner cartridge, which means I buy toner only about once a year. It's an awesome money-saving tool.

- **Pencil sharpener**—I do have a favorite pencil sharpener and I happen to think it's the world's best. After going through more than 5 electric sharpeners and seriously wanting to just get an old-fashioned crank sharpener to hang on the wall, I bought this one as a last resort. A homeschooling mom of 4 recommended it and I'm telling you, she was right. It has been a workhorse in our home for over 3 years without even a hiccup. Most of the other sharpeners were lucky to last 2 months. Trust me, it's a keeper! *(http://amzn.to/1xjkzbH)*

My annual shopping list usually looks like this:

- **Ticonderoga pencils**—yes I am a brand snob on this one. Once I switched to these pencils and stopped buying the cheap versions, I always found that at the end of the year, we STILL had pencils. They weren't all broken or missing erasers anymore. I promise, you won't go back to other brands. *(http://amzn.to/113QBga)*
- **Glue sticks**—generally 5 per elementary student, 20-30 for a kindergartner or preschooler
- **Bottles of glue**—we buy about 5 per year for the whole family.
- **Notebooks**—I buy 1.5 inch notebooks for each child.
- **Computer paper**—we can easily go through 10 packs of this a year. I find that it goes on sale at Walmart often enough I don't need to buy that many at a time.
- **Wooden rulers**—1 per student. I buy wooden only because the plastic ones usually don't have all the measurements on them.
- **Big pink erasers**—3 or 4 per student
- **Crayons**—5 boxes per elementary student, 10 boxes for a kindergartner or preschooler. You want to buy these

during the sales, as they are significantly cheaper. You can always save what you don't use for next year.

- **Colored pencils**—4-5 packs per student. I really prefer for my kids to use these over crayons and markers when they are notebooking. The pencils are much neater and don't bleed.

And that's it. I try not to purchase too much, but I'd rather be over than under. A shortage on crayons would cost me nearly 200% more if I bought them in the spring instead of at back-to-school time. Plus, crayons never go bad!

Writing Your Mission

Before we go any further with setting up your homeschool, you need a mission. Personally, I'd be tempted to skip this part. How's that for transparency? Somehow, between the million things I do every day, I simply fail to plan. I think it's because I am so busy that I figure the long-range planning part is something I can skip to save time. That is such an incredible lie! Not laying a foundation will not save you time, it will cost you! So let me preach to myself (and anyone else who really wanted to skip this chapter).

Goal setting is the single common thread in successful businesses and individuals. Did you read that? Successfully accomplishing something looks different from one company/

person to the next, but the foundation of that success is a mission statement and goals. It's been proven countless times. Of course, as Christians we have something even larger than that. The Bible says that if you commit your work to the Lord, your plans will be established (Prov. 16:3). I don't know about you, but I find that very comforting!

simple and practical homeschool room

www.notconsumed.com

So let's apply these thoughts to homeschooling. You might be wondering how a mission statement and goals could possibly help you have a successful homeschool. A lot of homeschoolers blow it off and claim that their mission and goal is to get the high school diploma. But that's not specific enough! There are multiple ways to get to that goal. We need to narrow the mission in order to set attainable and specific goals.

Your homeschool mission will help you narrow down your destination. You can't get where you are going if you don't know where you are going! So you want a high school diploma, but then what? Will you aspire to college admission? Or opt for trade school? Are you more concerned with training your children to manage their home or to manage a business? These and many more questions will need to be considered in order to determine where you are really going.

Your homeschool mission will help you know how to get to your goals. I often find that when I can't decide about participating in something or purchasing a particular curriculum, I evaluate it based on how it will help me accomplish my goals. If it helps me accomplish a goal, it is worth the time and/or money. If it doesn't move us toward the goal, I may need to reconsider. Of course, if it HURTS my goal (and sometimes things do) then I know I need to stay away from that particular choice.

Your homeschool mission will provide much-needed encouragement for when times are tough. I know that times are already tough for you. After all, you are reading a book about homeschooling as a single mom. The world would tell you that once you get past this, you will be rewarded and you will find blessing, freedom, and whatever else. But that is a lie! The Bible promises that the world will bring hard times—to everyone. This side of heaven, there are always going to be dark days. And it's on the dark days when we need our mission and goals the most. Without them, we are far more likely to throw in the towel on the things in life that are most important to us!

So how do we go about this process of creating a mission statement and goals for our homeschool? Let's take a look at the step-by-step process.

Step One: Pray. Remember the verse I mentioned above? If we commit our work to the Lord, He will help us establish our plans. This is the most crucial step in it all. Take some time and ask God to reveal his purpose for you and your children. If you are still unsure about homeschooling, ask Him what He desires for you. Ask Him to give you clarity of mind as you think about the questions below and to bring to mind the things you most need to focus on.

Step Two: Use God's Word. Are there verses that support your reasons for homeschooling? I think immediately of Deuteronomy 6. I'd also encourage you to look in the Bible for help establishing your goals. What do you strive for your children to be? What should they learn? What goals does God have for their life— spiritually, emotionally, and physically? Here are a couple to consider: Luke 10:27 and Proverbs 24:3-4. Of course there are many others!

Step Three: Consider a Few Questions. This is an informal step. Grab a piece of paper and start jotting down answers to any of the questions that come naturally to you. Go over the list a few times and jot down thoughts or ideas—no need for beautiful sentences or anything.

- Why am I homeschooling?

- What spiritual goals do I have?

- What educational goals do I have?

- How do I define success academically?

- What life skills do I want my kids to have?

- What should our homeschool "classroom" look like?

- What does homeschooling provide that public school cannot?

Step Four: Put all the Pieces Together. Now that you have answered the crucial questions, you should have lots of things written on your paper. Combine those into a statement that explains your purpose for homeschooling. Then, put it somewhere in your house so you can see it when those tough days come!

P.S. It's totally okay to finish the rest of this book before you write your mission statement, just don't forget to do it!

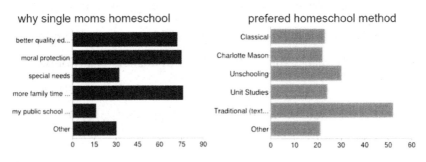

Single Mom Homeschooling

why single moms homeschool

prefered homeschool method

Choosing the Right Curriculum

Now that you have a mission, you can figure out what kind of homeschool curriculum will best serve your homeschool. Believe it or not, this may be one of the hardest parts of homeschooling. I've consulted with so many moms who were in tears over the stress of picking out a homeschool curriculum. It doesn't need to be this way! After talking with them, I generally learn that there are quite a few lies or "myths" that these precious moms are believing. So we need to start our curriculum journey by dispelling some of those well-worn myths about homeschool curriculum.

1. MYTH: There is only ONE SINGLE curriculum or method that will get your child into Harvard.

As grandpa says, there is more than one way to skin a cat. This is true for homeschooling. Maybe you don't care about Harvard so much, but I imagine you do want your children to succeed academically. Truth: There are many ways to homeschool children who will thrive in highly academic college environments.

2. MYTH: Your homeschool MUST look exactly like the traditional school environment.

Hopefully you already came to this conclusion in the previous section, but there is indeed a reason you homeschool, right? The idea is to get away from what is happening in the traditional classroom, not create a little mini-version at home. In most cases, these methods fall short of meeting the needs of students, especially those with special needs, active little boys, and, well, pretty much all kids. I'm not saying you can't have desks for your kids or that workbooks are taboo. You can have those things if you want. Just KNOW that you are not tied to those things in order to be successful. Truth: You can homeschool anytime, anyplace, and in any manner you desire!

3. MYTH: What works for your friend's family will work for you.

We've been thinking this since we were teenagers: whatever my friend has surely must be the best. Hopefully, you learned back then how wrong this thinking is. So don't fall back into it when it comes to homeschool curriculum. Just because it works for a friend's family, does NOT mean it will be a good fit for you (unless you and your friend are identical twins, share the same husband, and your children are clones). Seriously though, God has designed us all to be unique. Take ideas and suggestions from your friends, but never buy something just because it works for them. Truth: Every family has unique people, circumstances, and resources that will impact their homeschool curriculum choices.

4. MYTH: If you don't get the right curriculum, you'll ruin your kids.

There is no way to answer this one without stepping on your toes (I'm sorry). But, ahem...YOU can't ruin your kids if you walk obediently with God in control. As long as you have made a prayerful decision about that curriculum, leave the results in God's hands. Don't try to put it on your own shoulders. I must also point out that public schools switch curriculum all the time, some EVERY year! Nothing is perfect, not even curriculum! Truth: Yes, selecting a homeschool curriculum is a vital decision in your homeschool, but if you make the wrong choice, your children won't be ruined forever.

Phew. I hope you can breathe a sigh of relief now as we get to the real question. What is the secret to choosing homeschool curriculum that will work for your family?

Step 1: Pray

I don't know about you, but I can't rest in any decision unless I know for sure that God is behind it. I've learned this lesson the hard way. A little, "What do you think, God?" kind of prayer thrown in after I've written the check really isn't the kind of prayer that is going to help me. I suspect you've learned the same. Pray and ask God to specifically reveal to you which items to buy for your family. Ask Him to show you the answers to the questions below. Then have faith that He will!

Step 2: Evaluate MOM'S needs

Yes, you read that right. Haven't you heard the saying, "If momma ain't happy, nobody's happy"? You know it's true. The main point here is that mom is the teacher. If she buys a curriculum that requires 2-3 crafts a day and she HATES crafts, how long do you think it will take before the curriculum is in the trash? I promise there are enough curriculum options out there that you can find one which meets your unique personality. Don't feel guilty about this. Your kids will love to learn if you are excited about it, too. If you dread every moment, 180 days will seem like an eternity and you will long to put your kids on the yellow bus next fall. No matter how good someone says it is, if you open the curriculum and it gives you hives, DON'T BUY IT!

Step 3: Consider your unique circumstances

Your family's unique circumstances are a HUGE part of this decision process. Let's say, for example, that you are a mom of 8 children. Will you have time to teach a curriculum that is teacher-intensive for each grade level? Of course not. There aren't even enough hours in the day. If you are a mom with more than 1 or 2 kids, you will need to look for ways to streamline things for the little guys and ways to teach the older ones to be strong independent learners. This is the case in my home, as well. As a single mom, I work inside my home 40+ hours a week. Our homeschool day has to be flexible and my children need to be independent learners. There is no reason to sit and hear my 4th grader read out loud every single time, but every reason to do that with my 1st grader. I have to balance the time and so will you. So make sure you consider the dynamics in your home before purchasing a curriculum.

Step 4: Consider your CHILD'S needs

Of course, you also need to consider your child's needs when you select your curriculum. Do you have a boy or a Highly Distractible student? *(http://bit.ly/1x9YRII)* Typically, boys under the age of 8 cannot sit and do focused work for more than about 15 minutes. This would be very important to consider when you pick his curriculum. Likewise, maybe you have a 6-year-old child who is reading on a 5th grade level. (Sometimes that happens.) Until your child levels out, don't select a curriculum that will box the poor child into a 1st grade level reading workbook. Does your child hate crafts? Then don't buy a unit study full of them. Does your child love to draw? Then perhaps look for curriculum that affords her that opportunity. The bottom line, look for something that meets your child's needs!

Step 5: Consider the reviews

Once you have considered the first 4 steps, you may find yourself with a few good options. Now is the time to look at the reviews. Search online for opinions or ask your friends (if they've used it). Of course, if you still can't decide, don't forget to go back to #1: Prayer. In time, God will reveal the best choice! I've created a Free printable to help you ponder these questions. *(http://bit. ly/1Eq65sH)*

Choosing the right homeschool curriculum has a reputation for being a daunting task, but it doesn't have to be. Remember what we said in the last chapter about your mission as you make your selections. I hope you will consider what is best for your family first, but I know that you are curious what has worked for me, so I won't leave you hanging. My 2012-2013 Curriculum covers 3rd grade, 2nd grade, and kindergarten *(http://bit.ly/1EcAV6j)*. My 2013-2014 Curriculum covers 4th grade, 3rd grade, and 1st grade *(http://bit.ly/1vXh6LR)*. And my 2014-2015 Curriculum is covers 5th grade, 4th grade, 2nd grade, and Pre-K *(http://bit.ly/10ANMlr)*. I also have a work-at-home mom curriculum suggestion list here: *http://bit.ly/1xrCECx*.

Why You Need Independent Learners

You probably noticed my heavy emphasis on independent learners when I select my homeschool curriculum. Have you ever considered why this would be such an important goal in your homeschool? As an education major, the idea of teaching children to become independent learners was a common theme throughout both of my degrees. This emphasis comes from the workforce. Employers don't like to babysit; they need independent thinkers and workers to get the job done. There is nothing more annoying than an employee who is at your desk every 5 minutes with a new problem. We want to teach our kids to solve problems so they will be desirable in the workplace.

Another crucial element to consider is that independent

learners are independent thinkers. Thinking for yourself makes the learning your own and creates your own moral compass. It's no longer what mama said, but what the child believes for him/herself. This is crucial for helping your children stay close to God when they leave home. Whether it's a sleep-over with a friend or a college dorm, there will come a time when they won't heed mama's words. But they will remember God's truth that has been hidden in their hearts and molded into their character.

Both of those points are important to me, but this last reason is the one I most want for my kids: Independent learners pursue knowledge. When you teach a child to be an independent learner, it becomes a natural habit. As an example, after her school "assignments" have been completed, you will often find my 10-year-old creating assignments of her own. She knows how to learn something new and pursues her interests even without prompting from me. Of course, this is not a guarantee. Some children are naturally bent more toward certain things. Regardless, I think you will find that your child pursues knowledge as she gets older. You have given her the tools she needs to learn anything she wants to learn.

So how do we do it? Developing independent learners begins with home responsibilities—the things you do anyway. Start with simple things that don't cause potential injury; let them put on their own clothes. Who cares if it takes an hour? Let them carry in a bag of groceries. Who cares if only one item is in the bag? This not only encourages helpfulness and investment in the family, it develops a sense of responsibility later. You won't have that teenager who is sure mom is going to do it for him. As you develop those independent learners, there are some things that will help.

Keep your hands off.

You have to give them time to try. Back off, mama. Go do the dishes or pick up a nearby book to distract you, but whatever you do, give them time to try on their own. Walk away from the table, even if your child is 5 years old. If you ask him to circle all the letter "r's" on his paper, once he has circled one, get up and peel some carrots. Don't sit there, or he will require that you do that forever. I remember meeting a mom of twins once. They were her only children and they were 12. She was feeling frustrated that they couldn't get any school work done without her sitting with them. These children were bright, just dependent! I promise that if you hover—you will still be sitting there micro-managing your teenager's life. None of us really want that.

Don't give in to fear about this. Christ did not give us a spirit of fear. Your sweet baby might fall off the swings. He might get the problems wrong on that math sheet. But we can't prevent failure. Of course it's wise to be safe, but once you've taught your kids, revert to the rule—keep your hands off. Don't live in a state of fear over what might be.

Ask a lot of questions.

Questions are the key to helping children develop a moral belief system. "What do YOU think the Bible says about that?" As the parent, there is always room to bring out the Bible and show them exactly what it says. But allowing them to think about it and process it creates a habit for later. For example, what happens when a friend invites them to take a sniff of some white powder? You won't be there and you want his/her first thought to be, what does the Bible say about this?

If it's not a moral issue, still ask questions. Instead of telling your child that word she can't read, ask her to tell you some ways she might figure it out. Probe with your own questions to get her thinking about a possible solution. The more you do this with the little guys, the more you will find them taking responsibility for their school work.

Look for curriculum that doesn't involve constant mom time.

This one can be a challenge. I want curriculum that is solid and useful for educating my children but doesn't require me to babysit them through the entire process, especially after about 2nd grade. I want to be a resource and an educator, not a person who spoon-feeds them. This is especially crucial if you are a homeschooling mom who also works from home. Time is limited and it's wonderful if you don't have a needy curriculum pressing down on you.

Make lists.

Lists are probably the best way to instill the habit of independence. We keep a weekly checklist for school work. The checklist is simple. Each day there is a box for each subject. The child marks off if he/she has completed the next lesson in the subject. I don't mandate the order in which they do it, it's up to them. I do give some guidance to my 5th grader as to how much work she should reasonably expect to complete before lunch since she usually doesn't get it all done before then. Once their work is done and checked off for the day, they leave their notebooks and assignments open on the table for grading. Then it's my turn. As I have time, I check their work and assign a grade.

I have 2 simple grading scales. One for lower elementary (grades K-3): E= excellent, S= satisfactory and N= needs improvement. Starting in 4th grade, I use a simple 10-point grading scale: 90-100= A, 80-89= B, 70-79= C and so on. My goal is simply to help them see when they need to do a better job and when they are doing an excellent job. I do this in a very light-hearted way. I think grades are a great way to measure your progress if you can keep in mind that they don't measure who you are!

There is one last thing that I do with these sheets. At the end of the week, all "E's" or "A's" are awarded 5 cents each. This is the only money my kids get. It's a sort of allowance/reward I suppose. Either way, I want them to understand that excellent work reaps benefits. They have to complete the work; there is no way out. They are just learning that satisfactory or sloppy work doesn't earn as much profit as excellent work. I think this is a crucial concept for children to learn. It's not our mediocre work that will get us somewhere in life!

Here is a sample of what one of our weeks looks like. This is my oldest girl and she likes to color in the boxes when she completes the work. The other two kids simply mark it off as fast as they can. I didn't fill in the notes section on this page, but I tend to use it to write something encouraging. Usually it's something I noticed about their work ethic or helpfulness. Sometimes it's school related. I'm amazed at how excited they are to read their comments at the end of the week.

How to Plan the Year

So you've got a mission, a homeschool space, and a mountain of supplies. You've even picked out great curriculum that will work well for YOUR family's very unique needs. Now it's time for a plan. I know you've heard the Ben Franklin quote, "Those who fail to plan, plan to fail." Now is not the time to ignore his wisdom. Unless you intend to unschool, you will need to plan your homeschool days. But don't worry, there is a simple way to do this—simple enough even for our crazy single-mom schedules. Over time, I have developed a process for laying out the year. I pray that you will find it helpful.

Step 1: Pray

I can't make suggestions on planning a school year without pointing out how important it is to make sure you allow God to order your steps. He has great purpose for your homeschool! What I have to say is worthless compared to His plan for you. So start this process right. If you can set aside a day or two for planning, you will LOVE the results. When the kids are visiting dad or when they are with family would be a great time to do this. If that doesn't work, don't worry. You can do it when they are in bed. Whatever you decide, kick off the event with prayer.

Step 2: Set overall goals

Hopefully you did this when you set your homeschool mission. If you didn't, go back and do it now. Goals are the SINGLE most important factor of success. Do you have clearly defined goals for your homeschool? Do you know why you are doing this? Where do you want your students to be in 10 years? What do you want them to leave your home with? Whether you have a kindergartner or are a seasoned veteran of 20 years, knowing where you are headed is crucial, so don't neglect this step. I highly recommend writing down your goal(s) and posting them somewhere. When burn-out rears its ugly head, you can glance at your goals and remember why you are doing this.

Step 3: Confirm that your methods meet your goals

I don't like to put myself in a box, and often, picking a method feels that way. But a method isn't the law, it's more of a backbone—a support system of things you enjoy doing in your homeschool. Our backbone method is classical, but I reserve the right to use any method I like to get a point across! *(http://bit.ly/10AO0sS)* While I imagine you would like that right too, I would strongly suggest that you consider choosing a "backbone" method. It makes selection of curriculum much easier.

Step 4: Evaluate last year

If you homeschooled last year, now is the time to look at how it went. Don't move on and plan for a new year without this evaluation. You might ask yourself these questions: How did I MEET my goals? In what ways did I FAIL to meet my goals? Is there an activity, curriculum, or method that needs to be removed? Is there something that was lacking? Is there something I need to fit in so I can better meet my goals?

Next, you want to evaluate the students. Please don't stress about this. You just want to see how much progress they've made. Standardized testing honestly tells you very little about how your child is doing. Informal assessments provide much better information, and they help to identify areas in which you might need to improve. After I assess my students, I record it all on one sheet to keep for their records. I love this because there is ALWAYS progress and it's so fun to see. You can find various assessments on the internet to meet your specific needs. Here are a few to get you started:

- This Reading Mama has a great list of reading assessments. *(http://bit.ly/1tS6DVe)*
- State of North Carolina offers end of the year math assessments. *(http://bit.ly/113RhSC)*
- Assessment Tools by How to Homeschool Today has a great list of available resources. *(http://bit.ly/1soLrSb)*
- Pre-K Printable Assessments has several simple printables for those little guys. *(http://bit.ly/1Gzv3rB)*

Step 5: Set your schedules

I always start by setting my annual schedule. This is not a mandatory step because you can easily determine your dates as you go. However, many homeschool moms prefer to establish terms and breaks at the start of the year. They will also establish an official start date for the school year. Even if you school year-round, there is usually an official "promotion" to the next year's materials. It can be fun and helpful to pre-determine these dates. I like to use this Printable School Year Calendar and color-code breaks and holidays: *http://bit.ly/1uJRszm.*

Next is your daily schedule. Don't be intimidated by a schedule.

You can make one to fit your needs. Even if you prefer spontaneity, a routine really will help your kids and your homeschool function more effectively. Believe me, putting a schedule on paper does not tie you down or force you into anything. As mom, you still have complete veto power. A little later, I will share my daily schedule with you. Meanwhile, I thought you would enjoy looking at what other single moms are doing. If you need other ideas to get you started, check these out: To do list—Schedule or Routine by Amy Roberts, *(http://bit.ly/1shc1M1)* Daily Homeschool Schedule by Holy Spirit-Led Homeschooling *(http://bit.ly/1ACRlIB)*, Guide: How to Plan Your Day by Meet Penny *(http://bit.ly/1ygoIeL)* and What's a typical day like? by Confessions of a Homeschooler *(http://bit.ly/1uJRYgZ)*.

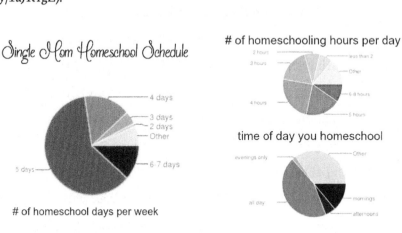

Single Mom Homeschool Schedule

# of homeschool days per week

# of homeschooling hours per day

time of day you homeschool

Step 6: Plan the course

Open that new curriculum you got at your favorite homeschool convention and get out the scope and sequence or teacher's manuals. Decide how much you hope to finish and divide that by the number of days you will spend on that subject. For example, if I want to complete Math 1 this year and it has 180 lessons, I will need to do math 4 days a week in order to finish the book by the end of May. If you completed the annual plan above, you will know exactly how many school days you have planned. But even if you don't, you can guess. I record this information in a spreadsheet where I list each course, the student's name, and the number of days a week we will need to complete that subject. Once I have this information, I can fill out the weekly checklist with my subjects and set up our homeschool notebook. You can read more about this notebook in the next chapter.

Step 7: Make a list of needed supplies

As we talked about earlier, the best prices on school supplies are during back-to-school sales. Take advantage of these sales by making a list of the needed supplies while you are planning for the year and organizing your room. There won't be any last minute fumbling for glue sticks and rulers in March if you stock up now!

And that's it. Now you've got workable goals and plans for the entire school year. Of course, they will flex with you as your family grows and changes throughout the year, but you will never regret having a solid plan as your backbone!

Organizing Your Homeschool Notebook

A notebook is the perfect way to track your child's progress through the year and keep a handle on their work. Many states require parents to keep a portfolio like this, but even if your state doesn't, I would challenge you to consider the value in creating one anyway. It keeps mom and student organized and ready for the year, as well as each homeschool day. Wondering how to create a homeschool portfolio or notebook? Here is what works for us.

The Materials

Of course, every good notebook starts with a notebook. Ha! Seriously though, this is an important choice. I've tried generic versions and I promise you'll regret it. They can't handle the wear and tear of a youngster opening and closing on a regular basis. Several times I have found myself going back to buy another notebook, basically negating the original savings I had with the cheaper brand. So resist the back-to-school end caps and head straight for the Avery brand *(http://amzn.to/1uIJki6)*. I buy 1.5 inches and it's sufficient for what I save. If you go larger, it will be difficult for the children to handle, so make sure you consider that. I let my children pick their color for the year. You will also need dividers. I am not partial to any brand, but I prefer the ones with pockets so we can store extra checklists and reading log sheets there (more about this later).

Decorating the Notebook

Every year we come up with fun ways to decorate our notebooks. This year we covered the back with washi tape *(http://amzn.to/1GzvFxo)*. We took 3 different colors and alternated them. Even my 6-year-old boy was successful in this without help. Granted, no one's notebook will go in the hall of fame for most exquisite artwork, but they did it themselves. I find that this makes them so excited to use it!

Next is the cover page. This is just a regular sheet of 8.5 x 11 paper. I prefer card stock as it looks nicer, but regular printer paper works just fine. We've done all kinds of things like decorating with stickers and drawing. I've learned that my kids prefer to draw their own. I usually print the page with their name, grade, and year. You could use a program like Pages or Microsoft Word to do this. I use PicMonkey and create a custom image (816px by 1056px), then use the font of my choice to write their names *(http://bit.ly/1x9Zimg)*.

What goes inside the Notebook

Section One: Daily

This is the section the kids use every day, so it needs to be up front and easily accessible.

1. The Morning checklist goes in first. I keep this sheet in a page protector and the children check it off with dry erase marker as they complete their morning duties. You can read more about how we do this part of the day here: *http://bit.ly/1GzvQc6*.

2. Attendance sheet *(http://bit.ly/1Eq6JX9)* and school calendar (printed back to back on card stock) *(http://bit.ly/1uJRszm)*. In every state I have ever lived, you must count and record attendance for 180 school days. I print this sheet on card stock and let my kids check off the day at the beginning of the school day. Here is my favorite attendance printable, *http://bit.ly/1Eq6JX9*, but the internet is full of hundreds more. Pick one that suits your needs!

I've been printing this same school calendar for years *(http://bit. ly/1uJRszm)*. I'm so glad the creator of this calendar keeps making new ones! As she suggests, I use different color highlighters to mark school days and non-school days for my kids. I don't use this as attendance because it could possibly change, but it is a helpful resource for them. Note: My life is full of crazy circumstances so I do NOT plan the whole year in advance. I generally will highlight a month or two at the most.

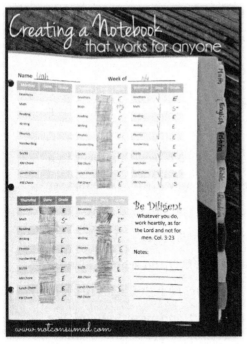

3. The Weekly checklist goes next *(http://bit.ly/1tKl1gB)*. We keep these in reverse order, so the checklist on top is this week's. At the bottom of the stack will be the first week we had school. This checklist is how I keep track of grades and progress each week. It's also how I assign chores.

Section Two: Assessments

This section is for mom only since my kids are only elementary age. This is the place where I collect pertinent information that shows their progress. Depending on how you homeschool, this section could look very different. Here are some basic things you might include:

1. About me sheet: This is our favorite first-day activity and it's such fun to look at as the year goes by. Here is a simple about me sheet for the little guys (K-1): *http://bit.ly/1soMvp9*. There are so many choices for older students. I created a faith-based one to use this year: *http://bit.ly/1xrEi75*.

2. Yearly Goals: You can find my favorite goal sheet here: *http://bit.ly/1xetOcf*. Another great one is here: *http://bit.ly/1tKlgbA*. If you have little ones, just write the word "Goals" at the top of the

paper and talk to them about what they might make as a goal for that year. Allow them to draw pictures and you can record their answers with keywords or phrases. Don't skip this. It's a really great skill to teach your kids!

3. Pre-tests or assessments done at the beginning of the year: It's great to know where your students stand academically. This was actually the original purpose behind the concept of a test. While I think that tests have become grossly misused, they still stand as a good measurement of progress. I always start the year by doing some basic assessments. This way I can show my kids how much they have learned. Here are a few suggestions: Preschool: *http://bit.ly/1wDi5VF,* Kindergarten Assessment: *http://bit.ly/1quJzGR,* Beginning Reader assessments: *http://bit.ly/1tS6DVe,* Dolch Sight Word Assessments (K-3rd grade): *http://bit.ly/10AQqYo.*

4. List of curriculum for the year: I literally just type out a list of what we are using for each subject, complete with the name of the book or whatever information I feel is pertinent.

5. Quarterly Progress Reports: My state requires these, but even if they didn't, the reports are kind of fun. They are great to share with dad or grandparents. Plus, it's a good habit to start getting ready for the high school years. Here are a few free printables: K-6 report cards *(http://bit.ly/1EcD9ma),* editable report card *(http://bit.ly/1xjnFwd),* Donna Young's Report Cards *(http://bit.ly/1sheIgN).*

6. Tests/quizzes (quarterly or annual sampling): I use this

section to collect tests that either don't have another place in the notebook or provide an overall view of progress, such as an end-of-semester test.

Section Three: Subjects

Section three is pretty much wide open. There would be a divider here for every subject that requires space in the notebook. However, not every subject requires this. We do many multi-age curriculum notebooks *(http://bit.ly/10ANMlr)*, such as science and our worldview study, that have their own journals. Here are a few of the things we do have sections for:

1. Reading Logs: I have my kids record every book they read. These logs are my absolute favorite and they are worth the money *(http://bit.ly/1xeuwGh)*. You could also do something simple and just keep a list like this one: *http://bit.ly/1wDiA1K*. If you don't like either of these, trust me, there are hundreds more on Pinterest. Just do a quick search and find one that fits your style.

2. Math: We have 10 small math booklets each year. Each booklet ends with a test that I put in this section. I throw away the rest of the booklet when it is completed.

3. Bible: We use this section to take notes on what we learn in our quiet times or to put in printables from the hymn studies we do. If you've never done one of my hymn studies, I'd love for you to check them out here: *http://bit.ly/1xeuw9g*.

4. Writing: My 4th and 5th grader both take IEW at a local co-op. We use this section of our binder to collect the best of their writing throughout the year. The teacher has them keep a class notebook, so for most of the year this section is empty. We transfer the best papers over at the end of the year.

And that's it. Pretty simple, huh? The bulk of our notebook is actually the weekly checklists for much of the year. By the end, there are tests and sample work from other areas to fill it up, too. I store these notebooks in a box in the attic and each child has a box of their own. Someday, they can keep the notebooks. Meanwhile, I have them ready to showcase our work from year to year!

Challenge 5:

Managing the Load

Finding a Workable Daily Schedule

Phew. We've come a long way, my friend. I'm so glad you are still with me! This homeschool journey is indeed a lot of work, but it is such an amazing blessing. I'm so excited for you and your family. I pray that you have found the strength and the details you need to make homeschooling work for you, but I'm not at all blind to the fact that homeschooling puts a rather large load of responsibilities on single moms. Take heart, we can do this! God has equipped us to do this. So let's look at some practical ways to manage it all.

A few years ago, I came up with our working daily homeschool schedule (*http://bit.ly/1OGIC7W*). It was based on the needs of my family at the time. One of the most beautiful facets was that it relied on chunks of time during the day. So if the baby didn't nap like he should have or if someone needed to go to the doctor, the entire day wasn't wasted. We could easily get back on schedule, even with disruptions. As my kids have grown, so has the schedule. I've found that we needed to have a little more structure, mostly due to my work schedule. I've also found that with a little less flexibility, my children can get more accomplished, as they are certain what they should be doing at any given moment. I've been testing it out and growing into it for several months now. The overall family consensus is that it works very well for us. So I thought I would share it with you!

Good Morning, _____

☐ Please read _____ today and record in your journal what you learn about God.

☐ Eat breakfast and clean up after yourself.

FREE Printable

☐ How will you serve someone today?

☐ Begin school assignments.

Satisfy us early with thy mercy; that we may rejoice and be glad all our days. Psalm 90:14

[Get this free printable at http://bit.ly/1oFW9HU]

In a sense, the schedule is still in chunks, although I haven't outlined it as such on the schedule. It still follows a similar regimen to the old one: morning chunk, lunch chunk, afternoon chunk, and evening chunk. The difference really is in the details we follow in that chunk. Instead of a loose list of things to accomplish, I've assigned more structured time frames.

Morning Chunk

In my house, an effective morning sets the tone for a great day. Trouble is, I don't always have time to run around behind each of my kids making sure they are on track. In fact, a few months ago, I was finding 3 out of 4 kids still in their PJ's at lunch and uncombed hair on a 3pm errand run. Seriously, something had to be done. Enter the "Morning Checklist."

I print one of these sheets for each of my children and slip them in a page protector *(http://amzn.to/1tS9yNJ)*. Before I go to bed, I set each child's school notebook on the table and turn it to the Morning Checklist (which is always kept up front). Using a dry erase marker *(http://amzn.to/1tS9yx7)*, I fill in the passage of the Bible that I want them to study and then the notebook is ready when they wake up. Believe it or not, most of my kids go straight to the table and get started as soon as they wake up. Of course, they are highly motivated by the fact that as soon as their school list is checked off, the rest of the day is in their control! I love that the Morning Checklist reminds them of the important things they need to do before they start attacking the school list.

The day starts with devotions, then the kids eat breakfast. As I've mentioned before, I developed a self-serve Breakfast Station that has literally saved my life *(http://bit.ly/1Eq7JKY)*. All of my children, even the 4-year-old, make their own breakfast in the morning! After breakfast, they complete the checklist of chores and then record a way they can serve someone that day. I never check to see that they follow through with this, I simply want to get them thinking about serving others. Lastly, they begin their schoolwork for the day. During this time, I am generally handling pertinent business matters before the school day begins. As the schedule shows, I get up a few hours before the kids and begin with my quiet time and then I spend the rest of that time working on projects and writing tasks that demand fresh and uninterrupted thinking!

School Chunk

I've done the school chunk many different ways. But in this stage of life, it's working best as a concentrated chunk in the morning. (Remember to do what is right for you! It doesn't have to be done in the morning.) I start the day off by teaching our worldview curriculum to everyone *(http://bit.ly/10ANMlr)*. They work in the accompanying notebooks as I read. Then I have a little time with Luke (pre-k). We will do a few pages in his books and read together. Meanwhile, Nathan (2nd grade) is reading his story to himself. Once I am done with Luke, Nathan will read his story to me.

(Teaching tip: It's really helpful to have your child practice reading the text at least once before reading with you. It builds fluency and accuracy, plus it will save you time!)

By this point, everyone is usually settled in with their school work. I work at the

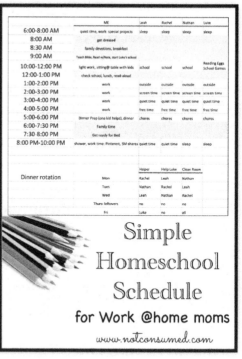

[Get this free printable at http://bit.ly/1oFWkTr]

table with them, answering questions as they arise. During this time, I keep my work schedule light. I want the children to be able to interrupt me if they get stuck on something. Do I teach them every single subject directly? No way! I've worked really hard to teach them to love to learn. I've taught them that they can learn anything by teaching themselves. I do help as needed and somedays that is a lot. But my older children (4th and 5th grade) do not need me to micromanage their lessons.

Lunchtime Chunk

At noon, I check their weekly checklists by grading the day's work *(http://bit.ly/1tKl1gB)*. Occasionally my 5th grader is not done with her assignments at this point in the day, but not too often. Next, we prepare lunch and I read aloud to everyone while they eat. We love missionary stories like Hudson Taylor *(http://bit.ly/113TAoQ)*.

Afternoon Chunk

This part of the day actually varies, but you won't find that listed above. On Mondays and Wednesdays, my kids have an "after-school" sitter. She works through the schedule with them, meets their needs, and keeps them out of my office. Ha! When she is here, I work in my bedroom with my laptop (that's what I call my office). It gives me concentrated time to make business phone calls, work with companies on campaigns, and create new project ideas.

Tuesdays and Thursdays are reserved for appointments, if at all possible. The 2 oldest have piano on Tuesdays, and Leah (5th grade) volunteers at a ranch on Thursday afternoons. If we are home during a particular time in the afternoon, we revert to the schedule. Fridays during the school year are co-op days. The children enjoy PE, music, art, and the girls even take a writing class (IEW).

Evening Chunk

At 5pm, the official work day ends and we head into the kitchen. Each day of the week, one child is assigned to help me prepare dinner. I'm so glad I started this last year. The girls can make most anything for dinner now. During this time someone is assigned to help Luke, and the others are to clean their room and work on chores.

From 6-7:30 we have family time. This time can be anything really...except work and school. Most nights we go on a walk around the neighborhood. Sometimes we go grocery shopping or run an errand. Other times we just read together or play games. I'll be honest, I'm still working on this part. Sometimes there is just so much to do that it seeps into our family time. Around 7:30pm we start winding down with showers, stories, prayers, and bedtime. The boys go down between 8 and 8:30pm. The girls stay up later, but must be doing a quiet activity during this time.

A good schedule should be simple. You don't have to micromanage every moment of the day, but you don't want to leave it so open-ended that no one is certain what they should be doing.

Managing the Mess: Chores

Growing up, my mom had one priority for me: college. She was determined that if I could just make excellent grades and get into college, my life would be perfect. In fact, she often made accommodations at home to make sure I would have plenty of time to study. One of those accommodations was that she rarely made me responsible for any household chores.

You would think that any person would be totally excited about this and I probably was back then. The trouble came when I moved out and got married. I didn't have a clue how to clean anything. I had never done a load of laundry. And the stove? Well, I could make rice crispy treats and frozen waffles.

I know you are probably laughing at the thought, but it really wasn't so funny. It took me years to make up for what I really needed to know to take care of my home and family. Of course, I don't say this to trash my momma for her faults. She was absolutely amazing and did the best she could, just like every other momma out there. All parents make mistakes, but a wise person looks at the lessons they have learned in life and sets goals to improve. Enter "Project Family Chores."

Why Should My Child Do Chores?

Chores are a valuable part of family life. I don't know about you, but I don't want my kids to miss this opportunity! I have my children do chores because it:

- teaches excellent work ethics
- helps you learn to work for someone else
- builds a sense of loyalty toward the family

- prepares you for life
- enables mom (especially this single mom) to actually manage the whole house

When Should I Start Chores?

I am so thankful that I started chores with my kids when they were very young. If I had it to do over again, one thing I would have taught my kids was to play with one thing and put it away. As a small child, this can be taught, I just didn't do it. Nonetheless, I did teach them a lot about chores.

It is indeed more difficult to do my own chores when I am teaching a young child. I can easily see why many parents abandon the idea. Many times it just seems easier to do it yourself, but you have to think long term here. Your goal is to teach them, not to make your own life easier. (But eventually you will get that, too!)

I begin holding my children accountable for chores around age 3. This is about the time when they are constantly asking to help and think it is really exciting to have the opportunity. Capitalize on that and find fun ways for your child to be involved.

A few years ago, our schedule looked a little like this:

- Nathan (4) was responsible for putting away the silverware, clearing plates from the dinner table, dumping the bathroom trash, and putting away his laundry.

- Rachel (7) was responsible for wiping the dinner table and counters, sweeping/mopping the kitchen floor, scrubbing toilets, folding ALL the laundry and putting away her own.

- Leah (8) was responsible for unloading and loading the dishwasher, scrubbing bathroom sinks, vacuuming the carpet, sorting and loading laundry to be washed, and putting away her own.

Today, my children are 10, 9, 7, and 4. All four of them contribute to the family through chores. The older 3 rotate through a zone schedule that I will share below. Between the three of them, they are responsible for the entire house. They do bathrooms, sweep floors, do all the dishes, wash and fold all the laundry, and keep their rooms clean.

The youngest child, Luke, does have responsibilities. He helps me with tasks as much as possible. He also unloads the silverware and dumps the bathroom trash. All the children rotate with helping me prepare the dinner meal each day. Breakfasts and lunches for 3-4 months are prepared in one afternoon with our breakfast *(http://bit.ly/1uIDxZR)* and lunch station *(http://bit.ly/1xjjfW7)*.

As a single mom, this is a big relief. We are home most of the time and our house easily gets wrecked. Having the children responsible for almost all the chores really lightens my load so that I can tend to other tasks. Their contribution to the family takes only about 30 minutes of their day, but it saves me hours.

Simple Chore Chart

I've played around with a lot of systems over the years. The one that I have found to work the best is really very simple. Our chores are divided into zones. Zones 1-3 are done daily. For a long time, I had a recycled piece of cardboard and clothes pins that I rotated through each zone. I tweaked and edited the zones until they contained an equitable amount of chores. Eventually, we settled on this:

Zone 1: Dishes and Counters

The person in charge of this zone loads and unloads the dishwasher, makes sure all food is put away, and wipes the counters.

Zone 2: Living Room/Laundry

The person in charge of this zone makes sure everything in the living room is picked up and straightened. This includes the foyer and the hallway to the kids' rooms. Once a week, this area must be vacuumed. This person is also in charge of starting a load of laundry and then making sure it gets in the dryer. Once it is done, he/she brings it out and sorts it into piles. Every child in the family then comes and folds his/her own laundry and puts it away.

[Get this free printable at http://bit.ly/1xtZJ9u]

Zone 3: Kitchen Table/ Floor/Bathroom

This person is in charge of clearing anything left on the kitchen table (including school supplies) and wiping the table off after breakfast, lunch, and dinner. They will sweep the floor after dinner and tidy the bathroom. Once a week the entire bathroom is cleaned (toilet, tub, counters, etc.).

At this time, all of the other zones are a group effort, such as the backyard and the car. As I mentioned, each person is responsible for his/her room and folding his/her own laundry. And that's it. I wish I had figured out the zone thing years ago. It has been such a help to me.

As I mentioned earlier, each day our chores are a part of our daily checklist for homeschool *(http://bit.ly/1tKl1gB)*. Once completed, the kids check them off and turn in their notebooks. I "grade" their work for the day, along with their chore. I do pay them based on this checklist. I don't pay them just for doing the work. As with their schoolwork, I only pay them for doing an excellent job.

Of course, if you adapted this idea for your home, your zones would probably look different. Your high traffic areas might not even be included in my list. I would suggest that you begin writing it down and little-by-little tweak it until the zones seem to work well for your family. If you need more ideas, here is an age appropriate chore list *(http://bit.ly/13U9enK)* and some chore chart templates *(http://bit.ly/1wNmaEG)*.

One last thought on this topic. I know you don't have time for a Martha Stewart home, but I will tell you that no one can help you with the chores if you don't have some level of organization. The kids will be lost. Friends and family will aimlessly wander, looking for a way to help. If you can find a way to organize things, the job will be completed much more efficiently. I stick with the most important rule: everything has its place. It doesn't need to be fancy or neatly labeled in file folders. It just needs a place where everyone knows it belongs. If you organize well, it will make chores much easier for your children.

For example, when doing the dishes, it is crucial that you organize your kitchen so your children can reach the dishes. We have one cabinet which is the main hub in our home. In it, we keep silverware, cups, plates, and bowls. Underneath the top drawer is where I keep all the plates. This way, when my daughter puts them away, she can reach. Also, the kids can easily set the table from this cabinet. A stool is also a kitchen must-have. Having a stool keeps them from jumping on the counters and helps them to safely put items away. Easy access means that the kids don't only unload the dishwasher, they can also get their own drinks for dinner and pour their own cereal for breakfast.

Another thing that has literally saved my life is drinking cups organization. With 4 little mouths, I was finding cups everywhere. Each time they needed a drink, they would use a new cup because they simply couldn't remember where they put the last one. Naturally, this kind of drinking created chaos in the dishwasher. So, I set out to solve this problem with the single cup idea. I purchased cute animal cups from Pottery Barn Kids. Each child has an image on their cup and they ONLY use their cup. (You could also use colors instead of images.) I have two sets of cups. They know that they must use the cup all day or they won't have clean cups left. This method also simplifies my life. I no longer find myself asking, "Who left their cup on the table?"

Believe me when I say that I understand the overwhelming mess in your house. There is a reason that I put this section near the end of the book. I think that sometimes there are season when mess is just okay. For me, I know that God wants me to focus on training the hearts of these sweet little children. I also know that I need to work to bring in enough money. So if the floor isn't waxed every week (or every year- haha), it's going to be okay!

Dealing with Exhaustion

I bet you know this girl: She wakes up at 5am just to get a little quiet time with God and a shower without tiny hands wrapped around her legs. She works 60+ hours to make ends meet...every day. She takes no breaks and has no days off. She wipes every tear, stays up until midnight calming the insecurities to her daughters, and comforts every middle-of-the-night terror. She does everything possible to make the leftovers into meaningful time with her kids. She pinches every penny, trying to find a way to buy enough to eat and keep the lights on all at the same time. She prays the jeans will hold out a few more weeks before the holes break through, and she gives her financial stress to God time after time after time. Her circumstances continue to swell into typhoon-size waves and she barely stands up from the last swell before the next comes crashing down. If it's not one legal disaster, it's another late child support payment. It's single mom exhaustion.

No, it's not that stayed-up-all-night-cramming-for-a-test kind of exhaustion. The single mom life brings on a whole new meaning to the word. It's more like I-haven't-slept-all-night-in-5-years kind of exhaustion. But it's not just sleep she lacks. It's emotional, financial, and spiritual rest she needs the most. I know you can relate. In fact, rarely does a day go by that I don't hear the same story for yet another sweet single mama.

It's true that God has specifically designed a mom to be capable of living on less sleep. He uniquely created us to deal with the many demands of motherhood. But He also created us to live within a family unit. He created moms to be supported by a loving husband who could pick up the slack or even offer a little nap. That was His perfect plan. And we single moms live outside of that plan, whether by our own choice or not. But, it doesn't mean we can't find rest.

There is indeed rest for every weary soul, whether it's in these single mom circumstances or a multitude of others. There is rest because we can lay every single problem at the feet of our Savior. In fact, God commands us to do so. I'm sure you are probably familiar with Matthew 11:28-30 where Jesus tells us to give HIM our yoke, or "heavy burdens," and take His in exchange. Perhaps it's because I've heard this verse so often, but I am ever-so-guilty of not taking it seriously. I've been guilty of literally saying things like, "This isn't really a problem big enough for God," or "God can handle this problem, but maybe He wants me to do something with it."

I imagine you've struggled with some of the same issues. **The truth is, there is often a disconnect between what we know**

the Bible says and the way we actually live our lives. I am so guilty of this. I can say that I trust God with everything but then I turn right around and try to figure out what I'm supposed to do. Sound familiar? In fact, I was pretty guilty of doing this all the time until one day I came across a verse that changed everything for me.

Psalm 127:1-2—*Unless the Lord builds the house, those who build it labor in vain. Unless the Lord watches over the city, the watchman stays awake in vain. It is in vain that you rise up early and go late to rest, eating the bread of anxious toil; for he gives to his beloved sleep.*

As soon as I read the words, I thought about the 4 hours of sleep that I mustered the night before. Did you catch how vain that is? I'm not necessarily saying that we should all just quit our jobs and stay in bed all day because God will take care of the rest. But the point is vital: **If we are laboring against God's will for us, we are just running ourselves into the ground for no purpose.** It's all vain. The literal translation of vain is actually "meaningless." Immediately I came to my senses. I don't have time to be doing things that are meaningless! Do you?

I'll admit, single mom exhaustion is a tough case. It's hard to rest when the circumstances are swarming and legal stuff is not right and kids are going to bed hungry or... you can fill-in-the-blank with 100 other things I'm sure. But the truth is, there is little

I can do about most of my situation. And friend, that is probably true for you as well. This is God stuff and God alone can handle it.

Think about Joseph in Genesis. He didn't deserve to be in slavery nor did he deserve to be in prison, but where do you think he would have ended up if all he did was worry himself to death about how to get out of his circumstances? It certainly would not have been on the royal throne. But he did work hard and he did it with a good attitude, so he was favored. This is a lesson for all of us—a lesson not to spend our days worrying about how to get out of this or even the next predicament, a lesson not to spend our time checking and rechecking the financial situation to see if maybe, just maybe, we could earn another $5 somewhere. It□s **a lesson to spend our days giving glory and praise to God for every little miracle in the moment.** Because the truth is, you will find them if you are looking. And then when God's provision comes (like it did for Joseph in the prison) you won't be too busy to notice!

As long as we live in this world, we will experience great trials and tribulation. It's time to stop being shocked by it and start facing what Jesus told us. Life is hard and sin causes it to be even harder. **But we have an amazing promise through Jesus.** In Him we have peace, the same peace that has overcome the world! What a blessing! "I have said these things to you, that in me you may have peace. In the world you will have tribulation. But take heart; I have overcome the world" (John 16:33).

Truths about rest:

- Psalm 62:1-2—Rest comes from God alone.
- Lamentations 3:20-23—Because of the Lord's great mercies and love, we will NEVER be consumed by our circumstances.
- John 14:2—God's peace is not the same peace that the world offers, but because of HIS peace our hearts can remain untroubled and unafraid.
- 1 Peter 3:4—A quiet spirit holds unfading beauty and is of great worth in God's sight.
- John 16:33—In Jesus we have peace. In the world we will have great trouble, BUT Jesus has overcome the world!

Before we say goodbye...

Before you close this book, go ahead and write those verses on note cards. You are going to need them to help you get through this journey. You are going to have days that are so hard you can't imagine taking another breath. You are going to have days where you want to throw in the towel. I want you to have these verses ready and then go back and read your homeschool mission. Remind yourself of the truth of your situation. Remind yourself who is in control. Then rest in His control!

One day, probably not that far away, you will see the beauty in God's provision. You will watch your children dance in the beams of His unconditional love and you will look back at it all with complete awe. It's hard to fathom, but the promise remains. God is able to do exceeding abundantly above all that we ask or think, according to the power that worketh in us (Eph. 3:20). Oh girl, doesn't that just thrill your heart?

I'm praying for you. Don't ever forget: God's got this!